How Frank Lloyd Wright Got Into My Head, Under My Skin
And Changed The Way I Think About Thinking:

A Creative Thinking Blueprint For The 21st Century

Global Creative Thinking Institute LLC, Publisher
220 N. Zapata Hwy 11, Suite 642B
Laredo, TX 78043-4464 U.S.A.
sandersonsims@gmail.com

Copyright © 2011 by Sandy Sims

All rights reserved. No part of this book may be reproduced or transmitted in any form or by any means, electronic or mechanical, including photocopying, recording, or by any information storage and retrieval system, without written permission from the author, except for the inclusion of brief quotations in a review.

ISBN: 144 996 1312
EAN: 9781449961312
LCCN: 2010-908563

For orders of more than twenty books please contact the publisher.

Global Creative Thinking Institute LLC.
sandersonsims@gmail.com
Blog: creativethinkingbook.com

*To my fellow traveler
along the uncharted path of exploration
in New Thought.*

HOW FRANK LLOYD WRIGHT GOT INTO MY HEAD, UNDER MY SKIN
AND CHANGED THE WAY I THINK ABOUT THINKING

a
CREATIVE
THINKING
BLUEPRINT
for the
21ST CENTURY

by SANDY SIMS

Copyright © 2011 By Sandy Sims

"While writing this book, I have often been reminded of Gray's remark to Horace Walpole that 'any fool may write a most valuable book by chance, if he will only tell us what he heard and saw with veracity.'"

Violet Bonham Carter

Table of Contents

Introduction	1
Synchronicity	5
Launch Time	13
Back Story	17
Answering the Call	33
Metaphysics 101	37
The Great Sock Adventure	47
On to Taliesin	55
The Die is Cast	63
Land	71
Caught Between Two Belief Systems	77
The Hero's Journey Begins	81
Back to Taliesin	87
The Project Starts	91
A Strange Thing Happens On the Way to the…	95
The Pregnancy Period	105
Construction Begins	109
Closing in on The House	117
The Universe Provides	121
Excellence is Contagious	127
The Neighborhood Rebels While the House Goes to the Beauty Parlor	131
A Masterpiece	137
Let The Retreats Begin — Visits From the Other Side, the Inner Astronaut and the Outer Astronaut	141
The Kahuna Link, Hawaiian Shamanism, a Catholic Priest and Apprentices To Frank Lloyd Wright	149
The Energy Of the House Raises the Ante	155
Reflections	165
The House Goes Up For Sale	169
Entering a New World	175
The Road Ahead	183
Epilogue	187
The Invisible Challenge	193
Authors Who Have Influenced Me	194
Samples of Books Written By Luminaries	196
Index	197
Acknowledgments	201
About Sandy Sims	202

"This world, after all our sciences, is still a miracle; wonderful, inscrutable, magical and more, to whosoever will think of it."

Thomas Carlyle

Introduction

I set out to build a collection of Frank Lloyd Wright's unbuilt design plans, thinking of it as a form of land art. It was one of those ideas that seemingly came like a lightning bolt, from nowhere. It was so compelling that I found myself extremely anxious. I needed to do something, and not let it slide by aimlessly into the cocktail-chatter abyss.

At the time, the early '80s, I was an advertising executive living in Honolulu, running a small agency, an alchemical mixture of challenge and contentment. Ideas were our lifeblood, but this had floated in from one of the outer orbits. As a student of expanded thinking patterns, I was fascinated by interesting ideas about our origins and what we're doing on this planet. Although I would think about these things until my brain hurt, I did have one abiding focus:

"Why do events occur? What forces conspire to bring ideas into the physical form?"

"Science of Mind," the developments at the Findhorn community in Scotland, and a host of esoteric teachings had all influenced me. They offered clear alternatives, if I would only summon the courage to test them or, better yet, recognize that they were already in play. When you experiment in these areas, eventually lab work shows up. I knew the traditional methods of "planning the work and then working the plan." Yet here I was, inching into the water of another model, trying to get up enough courage to just "dive in." Intuition, coincidences and synchronicities (the latter Jung referred to as meaningful coincidences) could lead the way into what Jung referred to as "a causal" reality.

Zany ideas are the stock and trade of the ad business. However, this was different. Like the call of the Siren, I could feel some more compelling force at work, so much so I was willing to abandon all sense of my known world and enter the shark-infested waters of real estate development. It would bring me face-to-face with my own demons. I was too afraid to try new thinking patterns, but then I would beat myself up for being too "chicken." Consciously, I took the plunge, relying on these untested maps. I eventually accessed what I thought might be the magic and reality of perhaps a "parallel universe." In unimagined ways it delivered partners I could not touch, see, or hear. Yet, in some way, I thought or hoped they were there, in the "next" room, patiently and persistently trying to make contact: to let me know I was on the right track.

Overcoming fear in the face of challenge is a common theme. On the surface it merits no special recognition, except when it is happening to you. I remembered Joseph Campbell's mantra, "Follow your Bliss," and wondered what agony and joy my Invisible Partners had in store for me.

I realized that my life had been continuously involved with breaks, coincidences, luck, and disasters. Yet I gradually woke up to the idea that other allied forces were at work. The more I recognized and connected with them, the more magical things became. The more we hear each other's similar stories, the more we can accept the reality of these forces. More importantly, we can count on these connections to appear, to nudge and guide us. As time slips away in this highly technological world, we must trust more and more in this realm to preserve our health and well being.

My enduring question became: "If I abandon linear thinking, will the universe really take care of me?" By sharing our own stories we may realize the "100th Monkey Syndrome": as soon as enough of the species learns how to do something, the entire species seems to know. We will have been magically transported… but to where?

Here is my story.

*"Nothing happens by chance,
my friend... No such thing as luck.
A meaning behind every little thing,
and such a meaning behind this.
Part for you, part for me,
may not see it all real clear right
now, but we will, before long."*

Richard Bach

Synchronicity

I flew in from Hawaii to spend Christmas of 1983 with my mom and her husband, Al, in Tallahassee, Florida. There I had so many memories of a wonderful youth. With no industry, two universities and a state capital, the predominantly middle-class town was like a flower coming into bloom. Prosperity and the American Dream seemed to have found their best expression among the rolling oak hills of this oasis. The world could be ours if we just studied hard and unquestionably followed our teachers' and parents' commands. The town had not yet grown to a city. Lakes and woodlands bordered neighborhoods. We lost afternoons fishing, hunting, and exploring. Yet in an eye-blink, I could be back to paved roads, chrome-laden cars, ten-cent movies and lots of homework. Life was good. There was a buzz. People were getting ahead. We didn't have a freezer, but Billy's house had one. I can remember him opening it up, showing me the pot with last week's stew ready to go for another meal. Lane, the kid a few doors down, his daddy was the first to get a television set. I got invited regularly to watch the Red Skelton show. Soon Mom's meager alimony got us one of these marvelous boxes. At first we had a '51 black Ford. Stick shift, no radio. No heater.

"A car's just transportation," I can still hear her saying with conviction.

Four years later there was a brand new four-door Chevy out front, V8, heater, and automatic transmission, but still no radio. She was in real estate. You had to have a better car for showing those clients around. Not too many years passed and there was a Buick Skylark convertible sitting in the garage. It was loaded. Everything: air conditioning, radio, heater, automatic transmission and whitewalls.

"Whose is that?" I exclaimed, coming through the front door.

"Mine," she said.

"What happened to 'a car's just transportation?'"

"Changed my mind."

I had no idea how big those words would be some day.

Within a decade, these cars would represent the wave of an American prosperity we were all joyously riding, with the faith it would continue.

These were my thoughts as I cruised out of town from Mom's, down Highway 19, to ring in the New Year with my dad. At 41, I was a product of one of those early-divorce "achieving" families of the '50s. The taint of "divorcee" was an acceptable price for Mom, who would not knuckle under to the dictates of my father's domineering parents. It's a nice drive from Tallahassee to New Port Richey, along Florida's upper west coast. I had done it at least a hundred times. You'd leave the rolling hills of north Florida and pass through pecan-growing country into Perry. About three hours further down the road was New Port Richey.

My grandfather, G.R., founded this town in the earlier part of the twentieth Century. The Pithlachascotee River snakes through it, emptying into the Gulf of Mexico. Old homes line the wooded meandering river drive. Occasional fishermen dot the shores, throwing long high leads almost across the river, trying to snag a mullet. In the early days, this was the main drive, ending up in the town center and Sims Park. It was, years ago, a quaint Florida town just a few miles up the road from Tarpon Springs, the sponge capital of Florida. By 1983, like most other coastal towns, it had grown haphazardly, with strip malls, four-lane highways and endless traffic.

My grandfather was the embodiment of the American Dream. You could knock him down, but he'd jump back to his feet undaunted and ready to go. A newspaper editor, real estate developer and promoter, he seemed to have tried it all. The Galveston hurricane of 1900 that killed 6,000 people leveled G.R.'s hotel and bank account. That was bankruptcy number one. A few decades later he had acquired office buildings in Fort Myers. His tenants failed to pay the rent. That was bankruptcy number two. Borrowing all he could get his hands on, and with the rising tide of the stock market in the mid '20s, he bought 10,000 acres from the bankrupt Port Richey Land Company for $30,000.

He gave a few of his high-profile friends like silent screen stars Ed

Wynn and Thomas Meighan, and golfer Gene Sarazen, river-front lots on the promise they would build within a couple of years. They built mansions along the river. Their little compound seeded the present town. Meighan built a 300-seat theatre at a cost of over $50,000, and a partnership of G.R., Gloria Swanson and Meighan built a luxury classic pink stucco hotel called the Hacienda, hoping to attract the west coast film industry. Many famous stars did come, but The Great Depression ended their enthusiasm.

G.R., undaunted, turned to the Michigan autoworkers. For $10 down and $10 a month, you could buy a lot in town and G.R. would throw in an acre in the country. If you had been sentenced to a life of mindless drudgery on the Detroit auto assembly lines, the thought of retiring to Florida and building your small dream house was a lot to look forward to. My grandfather's ship had finally come in. He and my grandmother, Beah, spent summers in Long Island, winters in Florida, and lived abroad somewhere new each year. Tall, with a glistening bald head, G.R. exuded a serene confidence. We never really spent any time together because he was way too busy for that. Beah was like a doll. She had a beautiful figure and was meant to be seen and not heard. As a youngster, I used to love to dine with her (that is, as soon as I was deemed old enough, around seven, to be "well-behaved"). She would sit at the end of a huge dining room table. It could seat twelve, maybe more. George, the cook, would fry up a stack of pork chops, and she would delight in letting them dangle off her fork on to my plate one at a time. As a growing boy, I inhaled them. We liked one another, probably because neither one of us really had a say in anything. She was supposed to look good and did. I was supposed to be growing up without causing any problems. I did.

My dad, short and by then mostly bald, with a few strands he artfully brushed back, had a paunch to memorialize countless years of good living. He was perpetually ready for a cocktail or gin rummy game. Just before a party, you could always catch him in the back den or bedroom, reviewing his flip chart of favorite jokes. He loved to engage people. An avid student of economics and politics, Dad had been bundled off to Mercersburg Academy, then Princeton, and given all the tools for success. While I never knew too much about his youth, I knew that he had worked on a freighter one summer and had made his own racecar. A gifted writer, Dad could never summon the courage to follow his calling if it took him too far afield from G.R. and Beah. As an only child, the veiled threat of being disinherited if he didn't stick close by took its toll on both him and Mom. Dad and I were great buddies. The long reach of my grandparents' world was finally too much for Mom. She was able to convince Dad that their life belonged to them, not his parents. To appease her, he asked, "Where do you want to live?" Getting out the atlas she tossed it open and pointed. "As far away from your parents as possible; Seattle will do just fine." Dad mustered the courage to move. I was born there in the summer of 1942.

Within a year, Dad, who by then was working for Boeing, was transferred to Los Angeles. We lived in the middle of Hollywood. Mom loved it. This was the land of opportunity, fresh ideas, and great weather. She had an innate sense of design, loved to refurbish and decorate and knew that she was home there. She and Dad made friends with struggling actors and some of my grandfather's pals. I was too young to remember much. Years later, she told me that I was the first baby that Robert Wagner ever held. (I haven't trusted a movie star since.) Eventually G.R. and Beah appeared on the scene, as the War ended, imploring dad to come back to Florida and get into the development business.

My mother reluctantly saw herself being sucked back into a life she had once fled, but not without a fight. She had been on her own since age 13, when she got a driver's license and continued looking after her younger brother and sister. Both of her parents died in their forties. Hard working Nebraska farmers. Mom said, "They worked themselves to death." Her father died from a ruptured appendix. After that, her mom just lacked the will to carry on. My mother, a determined confident young woman, finally made her way to New York City in her early twenties, landing a job as a secretary in a large bank. Unusually attractive, she had a gorgeous figure that was accented with long dark hair with natural silver wings, and an almost regal presence. In no time she became a Camay Girl, which ushered her onto the New York social scene.

Dad told me, "She was such a show-stopper, and I was so completely swept away, that I asked her to marry me on the very first date."

In storybook fashion, she did a few weeks later. But now some twelve years down the road her confidence and his lack of it had ended the marriage. It was the early '50s, when divorce was seen as a failure, one to be avoided at all costs. To spare me the agony of the arguments, tears, and disintegration of the marriage, my grandparents thought it would be a good idea to bundle me off to a Catholic boarding school. Nobody in our family was Catholic, or religious for that matter, and certainly had no idea of what a nightmare it would be. I am sure to this day that no argument my mom and dad could have possibly made would match the agony I felt each Sunday as they drove me back to that school. I was tasting temporary abandonment. I would cry, plead and sometimes scream, but it didn't help. I knew my mom and dad didn't want to inflict pain on me, but I was bearing my end of the divorce. I never saw a smile on a nun or priest's face, but I learned about fear and I learned my multiplication tables.

Finally, it was over. Mom and Dad decided to call it quits. Dad wouldn't leave his parents' protective clutches. He was unsure of his writing skills and whether he could make it on those alone. Mom said his writing could enchant the gods. She savored every letter he ever wrote. They really did love each other; I knew this even then. She couldn't go along with his lack of belief in himself, and she felt that together they could have done just fine without his parents' money. We all loved each other, and accepted that this was the way it was going to be. She went back to college, got a degree and felt equal to anybody. My younger brother Byington and I moved with her to Tallahassee and visited Dad when we could. For me, the following years were happy, with Boy Scouts, Little League, high school varsity sports and college acceptance.

Byington was a tortured soul. He and mom were engaged in a cosmic dance that taxed both of them. In the latter days of her pregnancy, she began to read the *Hunchback of Notre Dame*. The doctor, at Byington's birth, said to Mom, "I have some bad news. He's…"

Cutting him off, she said, "I already know. Deformed, isn't he?"

"Yes, club feet. Both legs will have to be broken and straightened out. He will be a bit of a freak, at least for a while." It was 1946.

He struggled just to make sounds, but wouldn't speak. Finally, at age four he spoke coherently. Life was a torture chamber for him. He was diagnosed as schizophrenic at a time when we didn't know much about mental health. First there were drugs, then electric shock treatments. When they wanted to use insulin, Dad finally said, "The experiments are over."

By the grace of God Byington had attentive and caring teachers and learned how to read. He was seven when we moved. Over the years his true genius emerged in the arts. "He is a gifted primitive artist," said the head of the Art Department at Florida State University, "but somehow he isn't drawn to it." He could wind electric armatures with no knowledge of what he was doing. His friends were spiders, snakes, and any broken electronic gadget.

The struggles continued. He finished the 9th grade, but was bundled off to the Institute of Living in New England, with the hope that they could make some progress with him. Not long after that, the family, distraught, committed him to a year in Chattahoochee, the State of Florida's insane asylum. He was subjected to a daily Thorazine pill; it made life easier for the attendants, but kept the inmates stupefied.

Finally, he was released to make his way in the world. And remarkably, he seemed to do just that. Mom did the best she could to help him find solace. He lived with a picture framer for a few years, and the discipline brought out his artistic expression. He was a natural at junk art; all of his pieces sold instantly to other artists. But no real satisfaction came to him. He drifted from one set of marginal experiences to another, including two years with "Bo and Peep," the legendary couple from Oregon whose band of followers sold all to journey around the country, waiting to be picked up by a spaceship. He left. Months later most of them committed suicide at "Heaven's Gate."

He returned home regularly to Mom, who nurtured him until he was off again. He lived in a state of innocence, where danger surrounded him but never killed him. We were not close, but were a family. Innocence was his guardian angel, one that seemed to be working constantly. At some deep level, I longed for this blessing too.

I had made the 250-mile trip between Mom's and Dad's countless times over the decades. These short visits became precious, and my dad wanted them to count. When I popped in for a holiday, or to visit, I was it: the sole object of his attention. He dropped everything, and our long periods of absence dissolved into the preciousness of the moment. We were great buddies, but he always tried to program me with some recipe for success — mainly to make sure I didn't repeat what he thought were his mistakes.

When I graduated from business school in 1971, I'd made up my mind: I was moving to Hawaii. When I'd stepped off the plane on Oahu as an ensign in the Navy in 1967, the scent of plumeria in the air cast a spell on me. I knew this was home, or at least home some day. Of course I didn't think this plan would be accepted by Dad's logically calculating mind.

"Well, what have you got in mind now that you're out of grad school?"

"Uh, well, Dad, I've thought about it. I'm going to San Francisco." The silence was deafening. I was waiting for the blast to come. Then he said, "Worst damned idea I've ever heard! Don't you know? Guys with law degrees are washing dishes! What the hell you think you're gonna do?"

"OK, Dad," I said, "I felt you'd really be upset if I told you the truth. But I'm really going to Hawaii." I waited for Blast Two, holding the phone away from my ear.

"Now there's a good idea," he said. "A new frontier. Probably some real opportunity." I couldn't believe my ears.

I laughed to myself as I pulled into his driveway late in the afternoon. He rushed out. The big hug and his great smile told me everything was OK.

"A man must consider what a rich realm he abdicates when he becomes a conformist."

Ralph Waldo Emerson

Launch Time

The air was crisp, blowing through a cloudless blue sky. Christmas was definitely here. We talked about my brother, school, and the usual family comings and goings as we headed south to Tampa.

The car turned into the hotel parking garage. We were on our way to a holiday luncheon. Some financial guru was waxing on about how to survive the next crisis. Dad was mesmerized by these hard money prophets. It was his way of being prepared and helping us if he had to, but we never explored the deeper subjects of life except by way of stories and advice. Dutifully, I took up my part as we both delighted each other with impending disaster scenarios.

"But we'll be ready," I said.

He replied, "Or will we?" We both laughed.

The room was remarkably full of mostly aging men, many with Christmas ties, Santa hats, and even some with plaid pants.

As the luncheon speaker droned on, my seat companion, a Middle Eastern man, short, but with a piercing gaze, smiled at me. His eyes conveyed a mixture of confidence, compassion, sadness and wisdom. There was a powerful energetic connection between us, as if it were no accident that I was seated next to him. He leaned over and introduced himself in a muffled tone. I missed his name, and a bit of the introduction, but I was too embarrassed to ask him to repeat it. "…finance minister from one of those small African countries struggling to make its way into the twentieth century," he said. We chatted idly in hushed tones; he knowledgeably, and me just throwing in sound bites. The speaker seemed to hold no interest for him. Lucky for me. The muted conversation seduced me, although I didn't know that what he was about to say would change my life significantly.

"Bone cancer gripped me at an early age," he said suddenly.

"It's awful being bedridden at the age of ten, but fortunately I had wonderful parents who made life as comfortable as possible. To cheer me up they brought me autobiographies from the library."

He paused, then slowly turned, riveting his eyes to mine, and said, "There are countless biographies, but the autobiography... now that's quite another thing. If well told, that is, if the author makes himself or herself vulnerable enough, you'll hear their soul speak — something no biographer can capture. The triumphs, failures, and the tenacious richness of their journey comes to you from a deeper, more authentic space."

There was a payoff here. I leaned closer, not wanting to miss a word.

"After a year or so of reading, I had an epiphany, a realization of the common thread they were all connected to," he said in hushed tones.

I leaned in.

"All swam against the currents of their time. They were contrarians marching to the beat of different drummers, every single one of them."

"Slowly I recovered," he said. "Even though one of my legs was shorter than the other I felt compelled to give this contrarian idea my best. Thank God. I was gifted with financial skills. I recognized and honed them to an art. Eventually I wound up with a powerful position. As luck would have it, or is it luck," he said with a confident smile, "I married a beautiful woman who was game for this upside-down life. We slept by day, ate breakfast in the evening, and took the middle of the week off. In fact, we did just about anything to defy the normal cultural patterns."

The applause in the background grew stronger. The talk was over. People stood, shook hands, nodded in agreement and satisfaction, but I hadn't heard a word the speaker said. A much more powerful message, perhaps a course-changing one, was still reverberating within me. I wanted to hug him, but I couldn't. My cultural bias held me in check, but I shook his hand. "Thank you," I said. In those two little words was a far deeper appreciation, one reserved for those messengers who might have traveled from the distant frontiers of space and time. He faded into the crowd and vanished from me, forever.

I always loved returning to Hawaii: fun and excitement buzzing through the plane, people anxiously anticipating a long-awaited dream, a fantasy about to take shape. For many, it was the trip of a lifetime. Lucky me, I was going home; home to the land of the bittersweet. I called it this because Hawaii is sweet, but the entrance fee can be bitter. Though it's filled with people who appear to be casual and laid-back, many have a fierce determination to gain a foothold. You must walk a gauntlet, prove to the local people, and the mythical forces, that you're here to stay. Time is both your ally and your enemy. Competition is fierce, and talent is abundant. Prices are high, and an island way exists that appears for many to contradict and confound reason. Fresh out of business school with an MBA, I had bought a one-way ticket to Honolulu over thirteen years earlier. Every year I flew to the mainland, to visit both Mom and Dad and their respective spouses.

Over the years my two partners and I had slowly developed a thriving Honolulu advertising agency. We were like a seed that, like so many others, had found its way to the islands and was struggling to become a life form. It wasn't Madison Avenue, but maybe better. We were in paradise, growing steadily through the alchemy of intention, skill, luck and magic. My dad was so determined to make sure that I found my way in life that when I was 12 years old he put me in three full days of psychological testing to see if they could find my latent talents. When it was all over they said, "Whatever you do, it will be a hard life if you decide to get into anything requiring a mechanical aptitude. You haven't got any." Advertising was made-to-order for me, and I could do it in my sleep. I don't think that I had ever consciously thought that this was where I was supposed to be. But once in advertising, I was very comfortable.

"Twenty years from now you will be more disappointed by the things that you didn't do than by the ones you did do. So throw off the bowlines. Sail away from the safe harbor. Catch the trade winds in your sails. Explore. Dream. Discover."

Mark Twain

Back Story

Students were filing in, one at a time, to our marketing class, notebooks in hand to settle in for another rote lecture. It was springtime in Tallahassee. Azaleas and dogwoods were in full blossom. Long, balmy days could easily sabotage study plans, yet there was electricity in the air. It was spring of 1970. Recruiters were on campus at Florida State University, and everybody was going for interviews. Gazing out the window, swaying trees and blue skies carried my mind elsewhere, remembering the comment in the hallway by a fellow student. "Hey, we're just getting a union card." He'd touched a nerve, one that ran deep. It gnawed at me. I wanted to be free, be my own man, but I knew that an MBA was an insurance policy for a job I didn't want. I was not here for the love of learning, not this kind of learning. I admitted it; I wanted a fallback position, something to take care of me in case I failed as an entrepreneur. I felt the subtle low-grade anxiety churning in my gut. Graduation was still a year off.

The door opened and a short balding man in his fifties, our marketing professor, ambled in. His glasses were perched on the end of his nose so he could look over them with a variety of approving or disapproving expressions. Dropping his notes on the table, he exclaimed, not looking up, and with a mild sense of disdain in his voice, "Big week here for most of you. Transition time is like that."

"You'll probably accept the recruiter's offer of a nice paycheck. Next come the wife, house in the suburbs, two kids, a dog and a station wagon. You'll go where the company sends you. Who knows? You may even like it."

He looked up, with a long pause, over those glasses. Then he jumped up passionately, head tilted to one side and finger pointing toward the ceiling.

"There's another option, not better or worse, just different" he said. "Take time to find your dream, where you want to live. Plant your flag. Make a stand. Do anything in the beginning. Drive a cab. Be an organ-grinder.

Just get there. Cream rises. You'll be happy with yourself." Most of the eyes in the room were glazed over, preoccupied with other thoughts. I heard him though, really heard him, and knew this was what he had wanted, but could not find. His courage had abandoned him. It was his plea for a richer life, the one he wanted and we could still have. His lecture left an indelible mark.

The Vietnam conflict was raging. A 1A draft card was a surefire ticket to the front lines, at least for me. Unless I took action, I could count on action being taken for me. I remembered reading a Stewart Alsop column in the *Saturday Evening Post*, where he made the point that the front lines of the Vietnam war were attended by two groups: volunteers and fatalists.

The best offense was a good defense. If you wanted to avoid the excitement of the front lines, there were plenty of other opportunities to serve your country. Anybody who has ever been in the military knows one fact for certain: you serve at the pleasure of someone else. You can be mindlessly filling out forms one day, and dying the next. I had no real concept at the time of past lives or reincarnation, but I used to have a recurring dream. I was a young Roman soldier lying on the battlefield, a spear through my stomach, life slowly ebbing away, and still lamenting about how my youth was being snatched away. Real or not, this memory haunted me.

With graduation coming up, I had one more year to figure out how to handle the draft. This was the summer before my senior year at Emory University, so I headed north, hearing about how much fun it could be to work in a New England resort. I found myself driving up to a seasoned but cheerful yellowish building, the Lookout Hotel. On a bluff overlooking the Atlantic, it would be my home for the summer. The hotel was open for six months out of the year. I thought, this isn't bad, but there was something in the air that made my eyes bloodshot. The owner's son-in-law, constantly drunk, became my ally. He sensed that I had an allergy, since his eyes were less bloodshot than mine.

In my dorm room one night over several drinks he said, "Sandy, you know why I'm so depressed?"

Silently I acknowledged the painful ordeal he wrestled with daily.

"I was a nuclear engineer just out of school assigned as a junior member to the design team of the nuclear sub, the Thresher. I couldn't believe the final drawings coming across my desk; by my calculations, it would go down but not come up. I went to my immediate boss. He dismissed me, and I lacked the courage to disagree. The rest is history. The Thresher went down and never came up."

On my first day off I went to a nearby resort, to have the drinks I was accused of having all the time. After aimless chatter, the bartender, whose family owned the place, told me he had just been discharged from the Navy.

"How was it?" I asked.

"Not bad" he grinned. "I ran the officer's club in Roto, Spain. "Like dying and going to heaven. Parties every night, fabulous weather, Spain, the Mediterranean, not to mention the ladies."

He walked away to fix another drink.

My mind raced, chattering away. If this guy could find one of those great jobs in the military, why couldn't I? I felt like I should serve my country, I didn't want to go to graduate school right away, and I was very conscious of the Roman soldier recurring dream message. This guy's program looked great. I could satisfy a sense of duty, have grateful appreciation for a good life, and not have to kill anybody while doing it.

I blurted out, "How did you get that job?"

"I graduated from Cornell hotel school," he said. "The Navy has a special contract if you have a degree in hotel and restaurant management. The only hitch is you have to go to Officer Candidate School."

I left with new enthusiasm. I didn't yet know that my desire to solve a problem could set forces into play. And what an elegant solution!

In my own backyard, Florida State University had a hotel school. I needed a deferment. A second bachelor's degree would not do the trick. In Tallahassee, I was told that I would need to see Mr. Bond, the head of the local draft board.

After a quick trip to the barbershop for a real short haircut (only one chance to make a first impression), I slipped into my navy blue suit, and drove downtown, rehearsing my presentation.

There, slumped over a cluttered old desk, immersed in papers, was a full head of gray hair. I couldn't see his face.

"What can I do for you," he muttered, without looking up.

I asked, "Are you on the draft board?"

Slowly his head rose. A smile broke out, conveying a great sense of pride and power.

"Sonny, I am the draft board."

Gathering my courage, I outlined my plan.

He looked at me.

"Done," he said. "Good luck."

This return home and to school was smooth. I lived in a wonderful apartment at the back of a two-story building. My private entrance led into a tiny but complete living space. A raised gas fireplace and double French doors led out to a brick patio overshadowed by a large oak tree. It was only a couple of miles from school, and my parents' home. Ideal. Hotel and restaurant management school was fun, essentially a trade school at the college level. The subject matter was useful. You could learn about challenges in lieu of experiencing them. One night Georgie, a gregarious Italian classmate, and I were having a few after-class beers. His family owned neighborhood bars in New York. He loved to philosophize. I liked him.

He turned to me and asked, "Hey Sandy, if you owned a bar like we have, and found out that your bartender who had been with you for twelve years was stealing from you, what would you do?"

I finished the last of my beer. "I don't know. Shoot him. No, hang him. Why, did you have that situation?"

"We had exactly that situation. Charlie, the bartender, had a neighborhood following. Business was good, but we calculated he was stealing a half a bottle a night and pocketing the sales. It probably put an extra $20 in his pocket. More important it gave him something exciting to do. My dad decided we could live with that, and never gave him a raise. In the end we figured that it was a win-win. Charlie wasn't going anywhere, and loved the game. So why spoil it? Financially it was a wash, maybe even better for us. Just because someone is stealing from you may not be a good enough reason to fire them."

What I learned from Georgie was more important than anything I learned in class.

To make school even more interesting I was a serving boy in the Delta Zeta sorority house. We waited on tables, humored the girls, and occasionally helped with errands or requests. Southern charm and glamour masked all manner of insecurities and chaos. I was asked one day to help move a bed upstairs by Cindy. Upstairs was definitely off limits for males, including houseboys. I walked down the hallway, peeking into the private domains of the "unknown female," and got the sense that the girls were rebelling against years of too much discipline. Their beds were unmade, and clothes hung off most pointed objects. If this was the tip of the marriage iceberg, I wondered what other surprises awaited.

With my degree, I went to Newport, Rhode Island, to officers' candidate school (OCS). It was eighteen very long weeks, a rite of passage. The idea there was to subject candidates to continuous emotional strain. The theory was that it was better to find out you couldn't handle it in school than to find out you couldn't handle it at sea. But I was not headed for a ship. The smart double-breasted dark suit with gold buttons and stripes seemed to create the biggest gap between officers and enlisted men. The naval officer's uniform was a dashing, romantic sign of success and authority, while the sailor's uniform with the "Dixie cup" hat, was a shattering sign of failure to the officer candidate. Failure at OCS meant swabbing decks as an enlisted man for two long years.

The first day was utter chaos. I had nightmares. I heard the upper classmen bark, "Fall in, mister." I learned that there was no independent walking, and I got into step with another cadet, saluting everyone. We entered the mess hall, a loud and noisy insult to any form of deep inner peace. I fell into the line, and pointed to food items like the cadet in front of me. With my loaded tray, I headed to the closest table, but I never got there. The whistle blew. I heard a shrill command,

"Dining's over, jettison your trays, fall in, NOW!" Outside, there were what appeared to be cadets: five, maybe six. Their uniforms were missing the cadet insignia and gold buttons. Their heads were shaven, faces pointed down to avoid eye contact. They moved lifelessly, pushing brooms. I knew they had washed out.

My gut gnawed. "Don't let that happen to me," I thought. "Oh God, I may not make it. They didn't. They were college graduates. How much different are we, really. What have I gotten into?"

I developed nervous sweats. There were two ways to wash out: fail the course work, or "gig out." Sixty gigs did it. You could get a quick 25 for leaving your locker unlocked and confidential materials open to inspecting eyes. A failure to salute. Dangling threads. Scuffed shoes, all constantly gigged away. You needed the Buddhist idea of mindfulness.

The course work was designed to overwhelm. Books were provided, but not real time to study. The idea was to observe, learn, and figure out the system. Meals were sometimes eaten on the run. Shortly after I arrived, a cadet in Foxtrot Company hung himself. He had flunked out at the last moment, and his family was to arrive the next day. With a college and law school degree, failure was more than he could stand.

There was no acknowledgment. Just silence. The system was working; weakness had been removed before it could do real damage.

The company officer for Charlie Company was Mr. Potter. Short, stocky, crusty, he was a "mustang," an officer who had come up through the enlisted ranks. This tour was a twilight assignment, the easy one you got just before retirement. Mr. Potter, as we learned to call him, was playful and gruff but had a good heart. He wanted to see his cadets succeed.

The blue Volkswagen I was driving caught Mr. Potter's eye. I suggested to him, "Hey, Mr. Potter, I don't need the car during the week. Give it a whirl. If you like it, I'll sell it to you at graduation."

"Capital idea, Sims, capital idea," he said.

Mr. Potter and I became friends. There is nothing like mutual interest to promote success, and Mr. Potter wanted the car. I just wanted to get through, and he sensed I wasn't a warrior, but a volunteer, willing to do my part by assisting those who thrived on being in harm's way. In this manner, I was a player, as important as the future hero. But favoring me would never put any man in harm's way. Unconsciously, I accepted that life had its way of bringing pleasant surprises. Mr. Potter made me the company "Guide-on-Bearer." I carried the company flag, marching at the head of all company functions. I could steam independently with the flag. No saluting and, better yet, no late night watches.

Potter called me into his office late one afternoon. I sensed it wasn't a friendly visit; there was a limit to just how much grace I could extract from that car.

"Shut the door. God dang it. Jesus Christ, Sims, pay more friggin' attention," Potter screamed.

"I found your locker open. Now get going. Oh, and by the way, the keys."

There were knots in my stomach. In a few hours I would take the first of two dreaded tests in navigation. I couldn't really eat or focus on anything else. This was it: celestial navigation. I had to pass, and my heart was pounding as we marched in and took our seats. I was in a cold sweat. I looked anxiously at the blackboard, copied down the longitude, and started looking through the series of books to gain my exact positioning. Got it. I plotted the ship's course. Settling in, I ran the slide rule, moving from point to point, and things seemed to be clicking. "OK, I can do this. Relax, get in the groove. Then... Oh, my god, it can't be!" I checked the calculations again: my course, right over a small island. My legs went wobbly. The bell rang, and I could hardly walk. A group of flunked-out cadets passed. Our despondent eyes met.

"Mr. Thomas, congratulations. You have set the exam record with a perfect 4.0," the chief petty officer said, with robust enthusiasm. But all of his glee was really reserved for me. "And you, Mr. Sims, congratulations also," he said, with a sadistic joy. "You also have set an exam record with a 0.4. You copied the longitude off of the board incorrectly."

Mortified, but not desperate, I knew there was one more chance. I was prepared for the worst. I wouldn't flunk out. I couldn't. I wasn't swabbing those damned decks, no matter what. If I flunked the course I could repeat the last eight weeks. Purgatory. Some cadets, in that situation, had quit.

Two weeks later, before the second big test, I checked into a hotel on Saturday night, our one free night. For 24 hours, I sat in that room pounding in the information until I was exhausted.

I remembered the Chief Petty Officer's words. "4.0 Mister Sims. Pass."

Graduation was the closest feeling to heaven I have ever had. Relief in every cell. I was free. Mr. Potter's waving hand as he drove his Volkswagen home is one of my fondest memories. Another angel had come and gone.

Next stop, Patuxent River, Maryland. It was a special Navy orientation school for those assigned to club and housing administration. The tendency for officers not going on board ship or to flight school was to relax and kick back a little after OCS. After all, the bar had been earned. We were officers. Yet, something told me, "Do well. Your duty assignment could hinge on it. It will be a part of your official jacket." Only four weeks knuckling down got me a first in the class. That came in useful.

Lakehurst naval air station was to be my first home base. It was famous as the site of the Hindenburg crash, where the large German airship caught fire while trying to land. Navy pilots liked to live on the edge, and it was infectious. In no time I was hauled into the flying club. The adrenalin rushes were a narcotic each time my buddy took me up in the T-28 silvery "tail dragger" with a stick instead of a wheel. I sat in the front, he sat in the back. Better than any roller coaster ride. Before I knew it, I had applied for flight school. In a week, orders from Pensacola, the navy's flight school, were on my desk. My god, what had I done? The navy needed pilots more desperately than club officers. Then I realized I would be a fish out of water. Life would be short. The echo of "no mechanical aptitude" rang louder and louder. I remembered being clueless on the spatial attitude portion of the exam: how you perceive the ground from different positions in the cockpit, depending on how the plane was oriented. But there was no turning back. Then, grace entered the picture. Orders arrived, canceling flight school and sending me to Hawaii with no explanation.

The plane touched down in Honolulu and rolled to a gentle stop. As the door opened, the scent of plumeria, the swaying palm trees, the mountains, and the ocean overwhelmed my senses. This was it! This was what that college professor surely must have had in mind. One more plane ride, and the plane touched down again, in Hilo. But it wasn't quite the same. Sleepy and wet; not the same energy. "Lt. Sims, really great to meet you," the officer said, shaking my hand and almost hugging me. Cautiously I threw my gear in the army station wagon and hopped in.

As the sedan rolled along climbing ever so slowly, the landscape changed from palms to thick dense ferns, scraggy trees, and mist. My heart sank. The officer in the front seat chatted away, assuring me that there would be plenty to do. He could hardly contain his enthusiasm... for leaving. Pulling into the compound, I saw a tasteless grouping of cream-colored military row cottages. My new home was on the edge of the rain forest at 4,000 feet, 30 miles from Hilo, and miles from tall waving palms, tropical white sand beaches, mai tais, and women.

I tried to adjust for the first few months, figuring out how to get out of this new life. Ironically I spent my time counseling enlisted men having a difficult time; the blind leading the blind. I began to write creative letters to the Bureau of Naval Personnel, begging to move.

"Dear Sir: There has been some sort of detailing mistake. What a wonderful assignment this would be for a warrant officer on a twilight tour, and furthermore..."

Then one morning the call arrived, "LT. JG Sims," the voice inquired. "This is your detailer in Washington. I have been reading your letters with great amusement. Are you aware there is a war going on?"

"Send me," I blurted out. I grimaced to myself. Too late. It was out.

Silence. Then the voice on the other end of the line, "I can arrange that. The officers' club in Da Nang is available."

"Got anything else?" I sheepishly asked.

"Give me another year of service and you can go to Japan. The officers' club and bachelor officers' quarters in Yokosuka are available. You can run them both."

"Deal," I said, feeling great relief. My prayers of "anything else" had been answered.

Within a few weeks, and without warning, Halemaumau, the huge crater in the middle of the park, began to erupt. Fountains rose 400 feet in the air, rivers of molten lava emerged, flowed and dissolved, all in this fiery pit. I spent hours entranced, legs hanging over the precipice. This was the 50-yard-line ticket to the Galactic Bowl, to church services in a different realm. Mesmerizing. Thousands of people poured into the park daily. I couldn't believe I was living here now. The stopover in the Hawaiian Islands told me that Hawaii was to be my future home. The once-in-a-hundred-years volcano eruption was an added benefit. What appeared to be a setback at the onset turned out to be a cosmic reward.

A year later, I was in Yokosuka, Japan, where I was Officer in charge of the bachelor officers' quarters and the officers' club. It was the Navy's 5th largest. I was instructed to wear suits and no navy uniform. It was difficult, if not impossible, to say "no" to a captain or admiral in a Navy LTJG's uniform. Four hundred employees attended to every little detail. Brass doorknobs were polished daily. A thought became a command. I didn't complain. I was a figurehead with no real responsibility except to be there. It was both a blessing and a curse; a blessing because without my involvement, it would purr like a well-oiled machine. A curse because I wanted to contribute. I developed make-work projects to earn my keep. I was never questioned, yet in the end, I backed off. I was happy to leave it alone. I was grateful; so were they.

Discharged from the Navy, I wandered through Russia and Europe, and returned home to Tallahassee with hepatitis. Limping along, I was able to negotiate business school with the help of mom's cooking and plenty of rest. Business school was my last delaying technique. I went to classes, wondering how any macroeconomics and big company marketing ideas were going to be of any value to me. It seemed like so much useless theory, until I got a whim to take an elective, a course in Techniques of Financial Analysis. The professor, Dr. Griswold, was a crusty old man who had taken a sabbatical from the business school at Dartmouth. He'd been on Wall Street, as a financier. There were only eight of us in the class. Why was it so small?

A classmate said to me in a condescending manner, "What in hell are you doing in here? No one takes this course for an elective. It's required for a PhD."

It was too late to drop out now. The midterm was a day of reckoning. I gasped, "What the #%$&!" I could have been looking at Egyptian hieroglyphics. We were asked, as a company comptroller, to consider whether or not to use any of seven bond offerings. The mumbo-jumbo details were fatal. I was in over my head, way over, and feeling like I was drowning. All I could do was make short incoherent statements that added up to absolutely nothing. The blue book came back with a "D-," and a note that said, "See me."

He looked coolly at me and then said in a partially annoyed way, "You're not doing the work. I assign two cases a week and expect a minimum of fifteen hours to be spent on each case." He was right. Even though I was taking four courses, if I didn't bear down in this course I wouldn't be in graduate school. From then on, he began each class by turning to me. "And Mister Sims how did you…" At first I hesitated. He made a mark in his book and called on someone else. My courage awakened. Words rolled off my tongue with conviction, as if my analysis was right, at least worth listening to. The final exam arrived, the best I had ever seen. It was a slice of real life. Two brothers owned a large grocery store. A big motel on the edge of town was for sale. Should they buy it? Correspondence flew back and forth between them, citing selling reasons and details. There were a slew of financials to sort through. By this time, my responses were automatic: I knew how and what to look at first, how to assess the brothers' financial condition. Did it make any sense for them to even consider this expansion? Confidently, numbers seem to flow from my pencil. Then, there were the emotional considerations. Why should they want to venture into another kind of business? In the end there was no right or wrong answer, just the logic of our thought processes, with numbers and arguments to back them up. I passed the exam, and passed the course. More importantly I entered the course like a wimpy recruit reporting to marine boot camp. I left hardened and armed with invaluable tools for the years to come. Thank you, Dr. Griswold.

With an MBA in hand, it was time. I had put off making my way in the world for as long as I could. It was not about getting a job, it was about becoming an entrepreneur. I didn't want to work for someone else; I wanted to succeed on my own terms. My father's decision to give up his heart's desire to work in the family real estate development firm haunted me. I was doing the work for both of us, now. I bought a one-way ticket to Honolulu, the Hawaii I had only glimpsed but never known. It was my time.

Jim Swager, a navy buddy, offered to share a house with me on Maunalani Heights. It needed a paint job, but the view to the ocean was captivating. I saw koi in the fishpond as I climbed the winding steps. It was home. I bought an old battleship grey BMW 1600 with a pinhole leak in the radiator. I needed an income; any job for the present, but nobody wanted to give you a job until they were sure you were going to stay. So many people came to Hawaii only to be overcome with "rock fever," the high cost of living, and the long distance from family on the mainland.

Gentle trade winds, blue skies, waving palm trees, and the ever-present ocean made Honolulu intoxicating. Nighttime Waikiki, from a high distance, looked like a permanently docked large cruise ship. The green Koolau Mountains formed a backdrop to the compact city, with the ocean and beaches in the foreground. It was beautiful, and tourists were happy. The residents were casual but had a strong work ethic. It was relaxed and vibrant. I could see why people wanted this.

"Sandy, we'd like for you to join us," the pleasant bank officer said. "Let me show you where you'll be working." The job offer was in the credit department. When the door opened, a sea of lifeless faces poring over reams of paper overwhelmed me. My stomach tightened. Then, a voice said in my head, "No, no! Get the hell out of here." Back on the street the air was cool and refreshing, as if I had left the cosmic principal's office after a strong warning.

A pinball works its way down before it disappears into "No score." The rest of the summer was like that. Real estate sales looked tempting. Maybe retail. Lots of folks were in small operations selling everything to tourists. Did I want to cut my teeth there? Then, just as the September school year was beginning, a telephone call came. Leeward Community College desperately needed a lecturer. A teacher had dropped out at the last minute.

"Is this Sanderson Sims?"

"Yes, it is."

"We need a lecturer beginning tomorrow. Are you interested?"

"Well, yes I am. What will I be teaching?" I asked confidently, hiding the fact that I desperately needed to connect.

"Introductory management."

"I'm not prepared," I said.

"Neither are they," the voice answered. "Just show up. You'll figure it out as you go."

A break at last. Yes! I taught at the junior college. It was a toe-hold, with flexibility and time to pursue other things. I thought that maybe that MBA was worth something, after all.

My first creative inspiration was a discount book with offerings from various merchants aimed at the growing Japanese market. Had I thought it through? No, but during the next four months, I signed up folks, focusing on selling the final book to the Japanese Tourist Bureau. My concept was simple: the book of coupons, called "Money Off" would offer substantial discounts to the holder. It would be worth at least a small value per book. Finally, my moment of truth arrived. I entered the large conference room. Huddled at the far end of a 20-foot conference table sat four diminutive and bespectacled Japanese men. Within the first few minutes of my pitch, smiles appeared on their faces. I thought to myself, "Wow, great. Finally a break." I finished the presentation. They thanked me profusely and asked me to wait. I felt elated, patting myself on the back for a job well done. A few moments later they filed in.

"We like the idea," they said. Intoxicated by that statement my eyes lit up as I waited for the details to follow.

"But we can't pay you for it."

I was breathless. There was nothing I could do. Four months down the drain. I'd made an assumption that simply was not true. Simple as that! Dejected, I walked out.

Yet, there was hope.

I'd developed good chemistry with Tom Sellers and Rich Peck. They had put my presentation piece together, and theirs was the hot new startup ad agency. Rich had been one of the bright copywriting stars on the horizon and Tom had dazzled advertisers with his novel pen and ink artwork. Dejectedly, I reviewed my first failure with them.

"We're just starting as an ad agency," Tom said. "It's been fun getting to know you. Join us. Run the business. Help us pitch new accounts. We're on our way with some good clients now. We need a business mind to hold it together. Yours. What do you say?"

*"The important thing is to not stop questioning.
Curiosity has its own reason for existing."*

Albert Einstein

ANSWERING THE CALL

The Honolulu Bookstore was my favorite haunt during my lunch hour. On this day, out of the corner of my eye, I saw on the bargain bookshelf, *The Autobiography of Frank Lloyd Wright*. For $2.49 it was mine. As a teenager, I had been in the house Wright designed for the Lewis Family, bankers who supported the arts. A fascinating curved structure, the house was almost boat-like. I never forgot it.

This was to be my first autobiography.

The initial night, I got through forty pages; the next night, a few more. I dog-eared every other page from then on. It was a surefire sleeping pill. I was bored, but determined to finish it. Then a couple of months later, and nearing the end of the book, I awoke startled. Wright completed a thousand designs in his life. Half of them had been built. What had happened to the rest? My mind was racing, stringing unrelated concepts together like a crossword puzzle worker who finally sees all the blanks fill. A collection of these designs would form a unique expression of land art. Wright was an icon whose drawings I soon learned had sold at auction for the same prices as those of Leonardo Da Vinci and Michelangelo. These were not just the unbuilt designs of an architect, but the seeds of high art, waiting to be germinated. This idea couldn't have occurred during Wright's life, because clients always wanted the great man to design for them. If I could get the right to build these houses it could be a different story, now that Wright was long dead.

I felt tingling excitement, stirring, building. My God! To see even six or seven homes together: that would be real magic!

The "sugar plums were dancing now." Would there be a synergistic value greater than the value of each of the individual components?

In the morning I grabbed the phone and called one of the city's leading appraisers. "A very interesting concept," he said, "but only the marketplace can answer that one; there is no precedent."

My curious mind lurched forward. My cautious mind pulled back on the reins. "Don't. It's too crazy! Too risky. Let it go. You'll lose your focus, and everything you've worked for. But someone will do it." My mind was a ping-pong ball, back and forth. God, it had been a struggle to build an agency. Every account was built on fear and worry; yet with every account, more stability came. When nothing was working, it was easy to chase different options, throwing my energy behind first this, and then that. But finally, we had a base, some good clients. There was income. Twenty-two people were making a living from the enterprise. Could I risk it? What was the right thing to do?

"Asking the proper questions is the central action of transformation. Questions are the key that causes the secret doors of the psyche to swing open."

Clarissa Pinkola Estes

Metaphysics 101

The ad agency collapsed a year after I joined and invested $25,000 my dad had advanced me. Tom, the artist, and his wife went one way, and Rich, the writer, and I headed off in the other. We'd been the talk of cocktail parties and gossip columns. Irreconcilable differences finished us. No need now for all that room, but a lease was a lease, and construction had begun on the offices. Half the clients left. Rich had a wife and three kids and a sheep dog with a big appetite.

My dad's plea echoed, "Make it. Make it for both of us. You have to."

I was dragging, coming home early in the afternoon and collapsing: I had relapsed hepatitis. But then something strange began to occur, something I had no explanation for. I stopped worrying. I don't know what happened, but I simply couldn't worry; some natural endorphin was anesthetizing my body and mind. My worst fears didn't materialize; the agency was doing fine. I worked half days and rested, and my strength returned. But as my strength returned so did the worry. In the car I rolled up the windows, and yelled at the top of my lungs, "I need help! Please, God, don't. Don't let me fail."

That weekend, a friend of mine, Bob, called. "Hey, Sandy, would you go on a blind date? The nurse I am dating has a lovely lady doctor friend. You game?"

"Sure, why not?"

I opened the door and stood face-to-face with a petite blond. Her genuine smile and sense of self-assuredness were like an antidote. "Kerry Monick," she said. It was an evening of wonderful conversation. We clicked.

"The operating theatre is a lonely place for a woman surgeon," she told me. "You're an intruder in a man's world, with no emotional support. You're not supposed to be there, qualified or not. Who wants to live in a world of professional abuse? I became a psychiatrist."

We began to see each other constantly, and the weekends served as relief from rebuilding the agency, though I still wasn't master of my destiny. Larger forces seemed to be in control. Her condominium, high up and looking across the Ala Wai canal to Waikiki's skyline, was enchanting. *Architectural Digest* couldn't have done a better job with the Persian carpets and oriental design. And it was to be my hospital. There, I healed.

Over the next several months my world opened and I could feel new circuitry developing in my brain. Help had arrived. I had always wondered what a psychiatrist did, and now I was dating one. It was a complete immersion.

Sitting in the hot tub one night, Kerry said, "Suppose your brain is connected to another brain on the planet. You live in different places, but your experiences are shared in the subconscious."

I was intrigued.

"Then, suppose that the two of you are connected to six other pairs so that all twelve of you are connected. You now have a meta-brain so to speak." Something clicked, some kind of resonating pattern. Something at the cellular level snapped on. It wasn't an intellectual thing, but a shift. Suddenly, I felt different.

The next thing I knew I was in a state of eagerness, like a Pavlovian dog reading the books she sent me. The first ones, *Finding the Third Eye, The Fifth Dimension,* and *When Humanity Comes of Age* were by Vera Stanley Alder, an English author. These were "warm up" books. I found little jewels like, "Why are ice crystals on your window panes in the shape of fern leaves?" Or, "If you place distilled water in a yellow bottle and leave it out in the sunlight for a few days, why will it smell like sulphur?"

The energetic chemistry with Kerry was sizzling. A certain physical attraction was there, to be sure, but that seemed to ride on top of a huge energetic other connection, as if we were long lost friends who had known each other for eons and were trying desperately to catch up. Weekends in coffee shops, bookstores, and long discussions were delicious. By now I was reading — no, not reading... studying — the Jane Roberts' "Seth" books. There was no turning back, and I found myself spellbound by an intellect vastly beyond anyone I have ever read, or spoken to, and certainly beyond my imagination. It was like being with a mentor whose IQ was above 400. The core idea Seth suggested was that when we think with intent, invisible forces are ordered into service, as if we were field generals marshalling and directing an army to do our will. Yet we live in a dense environment, among others doing the same things. Some may be opposing our intentions. For example competitors who want exactly what we want when there is only room for one of us. Or we are part of a large movement, such as a political or ideological belief. Or we may be attracted to a personal relationship when that person is not attracted to us and resists. By the time our big desires materialize, we can hardly attribute the outcome to our original thoughts.

By this time Kerry and I were discussing the foundations of human behavior from a larger metaphysical viewpoint. She told me that in her experience patients fell into two basic groups. Group one would become aware of their personal power, but stay temporarily asleep. In a few sessions they would awaken, take full responsibility, and arrange their thought processes accordingly. Kerry's job was to reawaken them, so that they could take charge of their lives. Group two would remain asleep. Their therapy was a matter of developing coping skills to handle situations that worked for one class of problems, but not necessarily for others. For them, therapy would often be long and not productive. It wasn't that one group was any better or more advanced. It was more like a choice of experiences one made at some deep level. One would either be enticed to switch on, or not.

It was one thing to hear this, and another to believe it. We practiced imagining parking spaces and elevators opening up, and then celebrated when they did. Simple stuff. The bigger tasks requiring longer lag times were still a mystery. It was going to take time for me to accept that my thoughts and desires were having these effects. I wrestled with the ideas of coincidence, complexity, opposition and how they worked.

Were these simple things just coincidence? What about more complex desires? What about ideas that opposed? What determined the outcome? Did the one with the least fear prevail? If I marshaled forces with my positive thoughts and intentions, what kind of effect would my doubts have? If there were other realities intersecting with ours, what forces exist? How did they work? And finally, how much could I rely on this reality?

One night I was reading *The Magic of Findhorn* by Paul Hawken, the story of how Eileen and Peter Caddy left the security of life in the officer corps of the Royal Air Force to start a spiritual community. Their gardens gained wide notoriety because they produced forty and fifty pound vegetables. Roses grew out of the snow. In short, Findhorn was an intersection of unexplained realities. Peter had formerly been a catering officer. Reading about him, I realized how similar our paths had been. I wanted to meet him because he was on the edge of a new frontier, one pulling me like iron filings to a huge, irresistible magnet.

Two years later, I received a phone call from Charlie Campbell, a friend on the Big Island. "Could you put up a traveling friend for a week or so," he asked. "You'll enjoy his company." That evening there was a knock at my door. Opening it, I stood face-to-face with a tall, tan, handsome white haired but balding man, in his late sixties or early seventies. The energy in his handshake conveyed power and nurture.

"Peter Caddy; glad to meet you!" he said.

I had wanted to meet him in the strongest way and here, two years later, we stood face-to-face.

The following week was a dream come true. Peter loved Hawaii, for it was a vacation from his world. In the late afternoons, Peter and I sat back in bathing suits, drinking Heineken beer. I felt privileged to be with an ordinary guy, on an extraordinary journey into the frontiers of inner space, who shared his experiences in the most humble way. One afternoon I leaned over and blurted out, "Peter, how do you do it?" He thought for a moment.

"I'm living one hundred percent on intuition. It's exhilarating and nerve-wracking. I don't know whether it's my intuition guiding me or my mind playing tricks. Everything I need shows up at the last moment. Most of the time I'm penniless, simply knowing that grace is taking care of me every step of the way. Sometimes I just get a strong urge to get up from a meeting and go to a particular city, not knowing why or even how it will all come out. I just walk outside, maybe stick out my thumb and begin the journey, trusting that my needs will be met on the way."

"The whole Findhorn experience," he said, "is about bringing a new paradigm of manifestation into the world. It is not a community, like so many, of escape from the world. People learn new principles, return to their ordinary world and put them into practice. Originally, Eileen and I had a pact: she would meditate and receive guidance, and I agreed to do everything she said no matter how strange or crazy it seemed, period.

"I'll give you a couple of examples," he said.

"Eileen told me to order eight caravans — 'trailers' in your country. We, of course, had absolutely no money."

He winced. "The day the trailers showed up from the factory, I was beside myself. Eileen calmly told me to inspect them. I did, and found little flaws in each of them."

"'Tell the factory to fix them,' she said.

"I wanted to scream, 'What kind of lunacy is this?' We had no money and we were asking those poor people to fix things. I bit my tongue, and told them we'd pay when all was in order. And of course, miracle of miracles, in the next two weeks while repairs were going full steam ahead, people from nowhere, and I mean nowhere, just stepped out of the blue and ponied up the funds. I was flabbergasted, in a daze. I just accepted it.

"You should come to Findhorn for a few weeks early in the summer.

You'll receive training on 'The Laws of Manifestation.' Then with no more than $50 in your pocket, you'll head out toward Europe for six weeks, and see what the Universe has cooked up for you."

He opened another beer. "There was this couple from New York. Professionals I believe," he said. "They told me their story."

"They had completed the training, and were extremely eager to get into action. By the third night or so, in some sleazy hotel in Northern Scotland with a damp, cold, leaking roof, basically miserable, they looked at one another. It was one of those moments of total unity, and they laughed as if they'd been conned into a journey by asylum inmates.

"'Are we nuts, or what?' they said.

"They counted out their remaining $37.

"'C'mon,' he said. 'Lets find the best restaurant in this town, and celebrate our escape. How could we be so gullible?'

"Anyway," said Peter, "they planned to have a big dinner; get out the credit cards, and head home. They put on their best outfits and headed into the town's top restaurant. They ordered a couple of bottles of wine and started laughing hysterically. Sitting nearby and alone, was a rather distinguished gentleman. He smiled at them, approached cautiously, and said, 'I am by myself. You seem to be having all of the fun here. Might I join you?'

"'Absolutely,' they said. 'Pull up a chair.'

"They were delighted to have company, but they didn't talk about the true nature of their celebration. By the end of the evening the threesome was almost family. The gentleman pushed his chair back and said, 'I have had an absolutely delightful and enchanting evening. More than I could ever have imagined. You both have been a sheer delight.'

"He put his arms around them and leaned in. 'Let me explain myself more fully. I'm the editor of *Michelin*, on an unlimited expense account. I'm reviewing the top hotels and restaurants of Europe this summer. Come along as my guests. We'll have fun.' And so they lived happily ever after for the next six weeks."

Peter's life on the edge was compelling to me, more so than anything I had ever done. Was this a map of the future for me? It felt that way. I wanted to learn how to be open and courageous like Peter seemed to be. For him these events were no longer chance and coincidence. They were patterns in a new fabric of life; ones we all could be destined to embrace. Yet even for him, there was the perplexing challenge he left me with.

"Sandy," he said. "It was easier for me when Eileen gave me the orders. I struggled with the sanity of it all, but never questioned her guidance. Now on my own, I wrestle with 'Is it guidance coming through me, or is it simply my mind playing tricks on me?' It's quite maddening. I search constantly to find my center. I'm still wondering. I consult psychics when I'm in utter doubt. Honing this skill is part of the journey."

By this time the Findhorn books, especially those by David Spangler on manifestation, were eliminating my evening television time. His tapes became my work companion on the weekend. David's monotone voice lulled me into a trance-like state, perfect for painting endless small panes of glass around the sun porch. Over and over I heard, "be 'on purpose,' set forth the desire, give thanks for the fulfillment, release it to the universe, go on with life, knowing it will be done." It was a short and simple formula. Did I really believe it? I wanted to. It was going to be gradual, like working up to the high dive board.

This seemed to work for small tasks like finding parking spaces and having elevator doors open just as I arrived. The big items were still a risk. I'd lived in a linear world. My goals were to reduce doubt to a minimum, weigh and consider the losses, and then, if acceptable, proceed. That had been my reality; it's how the world worked, at least for me.

Suddenly I was looking at a parallel universe with different rules. Both ways of thinking seemed to deliver, but the latter was infinitely more elegant.

I remembered a book by George Leonard called *Mastery*. He suggested that our life is like a staircase. We are given tools. There comes a life challenge, a steep vertical climb. We recover. Life smoothes out on the plateau of the step. We like it there. Then more tools show up, followed by another vertical climb. Each time it's more challenging, but we have more resources: enough to handle the task.

John Rattenbury with photo of Frank Lloyd Wright

"Everything that is new or uncommon raises a pleasure in the imagination, because it fills the soul with an agreeable surprise, gratifies its curiosity, and gives it an idea of which it was not before possessed."

Joseph Addison

The Great Sock Adventure

I began to recollect, searching for moments when I had, with some fear, wanted to do something to have the sheer excitement of the experience. My one-way ticket to Hawaii, the one that led me into the advertising business, was that kind of experience. I thought about a later episode. By the mid '70s, my patterns of advertising office life were in a groove. When I wrote, my shoes seemed to slide off. I had to quickly slip into them again when staff or clients entered. One day a light went on: What if my socks looked like shoes! I would leave the shoes off. If people recognized them as socks, great! After all, this was advertising. People expected creative license. My partner, Rich, painted wingtips on light brown socks, and the "Shoosox" concept was born. We stuck them in little shoeboxes, and began to imagine the next "Pet Rock."

Everyone who ever comes up with an idea imagines how wildly successful it could be. But the items have to be made, then sold, usually in large quantities, and marketed. This was a big promotional idea, so, why not? John Rowe, a local Honolulu businessman, had just had a hugely successful novelty idea called "Showermike." It was soap on a rope, and sold all over the country.

We had four good designs, and a good sock silkscreener was my next quest. I found a fellow in Nashville, Tennessee, who screened all of the "Snoopy" sock applications for the J.P. Stevens Company. He produced several samples. Rich designed a shoebox, and then we started the process of getting "design patents." These are stronger than copyrights, but the process of name registrations, patent agents and attorneys rang up a $30,000 bill.

I went to the first gift show in Chicago to sell socks, without knowing yet how I was going to produce them. Gift shows are held in large exhibition halls. Hundreds of exhibitors display to department store buyers and small shopkeepers, who buy at least six months ahead, for the holiday season. The booth was beautiful. Large photos showing the various looks formed the backdrop. On the table were the three samples: added to the wingtip were a running shoe and a tennis shoe. The little shoeboxes were the perfect touch, each with a photo of the contents and a nice logo. We got orders for a 1,000 dozen socks. I packed up and headed to the next gift show in Dallas.

The orders kept building. Yet, I was in a quandary. Tube socks, the kind these designs were screened on, were in short supply. Big U.S. companies like Sears and Penny's were at the head of the line, and small customers were required to deposit 50 percent of their manufacturing order, and pay the balance when the order was completed. The orders I wrote from large buyers such as Sak's had a delivery time window: not before a given date, and not after another. If the sock manufacturer delivered late, the orders would be cancelled. This created an untenable position; we had socks with no market, and 50 percent of the manufacturing cost was committed. I knew that a small customer like us was of no significance compared to a Sears or Penny's. If my orders couldn't be filled, it wouldn't matter to them.

The New York gift show was the climax of six long years on the road. Though I was out of money, with over 2,000 dozen sock orders, I was following my bliss and my intuition. Would I raise the money it would take to produce the socks, or notify the buyers that I couldn't produce the socks, and go home and quit?

Then, I received a call from my silkscreener.

"Sandy," he said, "I've got some interesting news for you. The president of the J.P. Stevens hosiery division wants to meet with you. He seems to like your idea."

New York is an electric city. The streets and sidewalks are alive with traffic jams, cabs honking, and people rushing to their next destination, all between 9 to 5. Business is the point; no time for any chit chat. The elevator ride to the top floor was a long one. This was Corporate America. The door opened. The receptionist ushered me into the largest private office I had ever seen. I could have put ten of my offices in this space. My eyes rested on the portly man sitting behind a corner desk. I had my briefcase, but he motioned me to sit down and said, "Put away your materials. I want to buy this sock to give to my salesmen as a novelty door opener. Sales are down. That's it. I'll guarantee you an income of $30,000, and a percentage of net sales after that."

He wanted to abandon my idea of Shoosox in a shoebox, an idea that was selling in the marketplace, and use the socks in a way my instincts told me would fail. I knew it was time to return to responsibility in Hawaii. Was I meant to abandon the advertising business for this one lark? "No, of course not," my sensible left brain said as it wrestled control from the right side. "But hold it," I thought, "we did get this far."

By this time Glenn, a man from Hawaii with Canadian contacts, had joined me. We licensed the J.P. Stevens Company, and subsequently another company in Canada. The adventure was over. They fulfilled all of my Shoosox orders, and then took it on as their project. The cost of protecting the designs had used up all of the money from the royalties. But I emerged unscathed from my journey into the unknown.

In retrospect I had been aware that forces had coalesced to send me on a training exercise. At times when my MBA training would have dictated prudence, something else urged me to step into the breach and take a chance. There was mindfulness in the exercise, and yet a gnawing doubt. No matter how much my intellect wanted to think I was being taken care of, my new life was full of anxiety. I returned to Hawaii and the agency as if I had been on a long, dreamlike trip. By this time the advertising business had stabilized, as much as it ever would, yet I continued to worry. I wanted to believe, but couldn't quite. I needed a steady diet of proof about how things worked in the non-linear world.

At the heart of it was my own perplexity about the nature of this new reality: the idea of tuning into hunches, feelings, the intuitive urge, allowing "it" to happen through me. I looked for clues, signs, and synchronistic patterns of meaningful coincidences that assured me I was on the right path. Was I part of a larger scheme in which my life's journey could be a partnership with other conscious forces? But what about free will, and deciding about the things I wanted, getting them by putting my intention into the universe, and then harvesting the results? I saw that people with high intention worked toward a goal and eventually obtained it. Then there were my own shortcomings, my fears and insecurities. What was my tolerance for loss? Yes, I could spout the metaphysical platitudes of creating my own reality, but how did I feel about risking ten years or more of hard work and material comforts, only to begin again if I lost them? What about lag time, or opposing forces made up of those who wanted exactly what I wanted, and wanted me to fail? If the goal were large the lag time might seem eternal. I had to find a way to align what I had found out with my doubts and shortcomings. The parking places opened when I needed them. The friends I wanted to hear from called. But if I wanted to win the lottery and bought a ticket, I would be competing with countless others with the same desire. Who would be chosen? What began to appear to me was that purity of experience was a key. If I wanted to win the lottery and looked at my deepest motives, I would uncover many insecurities. The winnings would relieve me of financial concerns about the future. That, however might only be masking a fear that I could not create in the future what I needed as I needed it. Was I sure about this? No. Did it feel true? Yes.

About this time, Neuro-Linguistic Programming was becoming popular. The seminal work had been done by two psychologists, Grindler and Bandler, and showed that the human species comes in three basic models for primary information processing. We are visual, auditory or kinesthetic. Knowing which way people are wired opens the doorways to communication below the conscious threshold. For example I am visual. I notice how things look first; if they please my eye, I feel receptive.

The phone rang one afternoon.

"Hi Sandy, its Paige. Want to go to Tony Robbins' Neuro-Linguistic Programming Seminar?"

I hadn't heard of Tony but I had always admired Paige. Blond, blue-eyed, rugged yet feminine, she had been Bob Rediske's girlfriend for over a decade. And, of course, Bob had introduced me to Kerry. Bob and Paige had coauthored the book *"Principles and Practices of Hawaiian Real Estate,"* and developed a highly successful real estate school.

More importantly, they were living a lifestyle I envied. Their work always seemed like it was fun, as if it were almost play: something that needed to be done, but not at the expense of enjoying life. Paige was an adventurer. She sailed the Pacific, flew the islands in her small plane, skied, rode horseback or traveled. She had grown up in the islands, and had had a strong upbringing in the Religious Science Church. At some level I knew her life was a result of these principles put into practice, similar to those from the Findhorn community.

In the next moment she said, "The first night we walk on hot coals." I paused. "Really," I said. "OK, I'm game. After you."

As we pulled into the ranch grounds, Paige and I both did a double-take. It was six in the evening. The mixture of anxiety and fear almost paralyzed me, as I felt the heat from the intensely raging bonfire. In just five hours, I was supposed to be walking on its red-hot coals. Fear is supposed to keep us from doing stupid things like stepping on hot coals. The synapses of my brain were at war with one another. I can. I can't. I can. I can't.

About a hundred and fifty people filled up the tent, and the energy was intense. Standing in front of us was a leader of the New Age movement, Tony Robbins. Young, brash, full of himself, but dynamic. My rational mind told me, "You can do this. If people were burning their feet, this program would have folded fast. He couldn't be doing this all over the country and succeeding." I became calmer. "Just get on with it," said the little voice.

Tony's eyes burned right through me, and his voice riveted the crowd, as he turned and pointed to the raging fire, saying, "Some of you are going to do something tonight you never thought you could."

"You're going to walk barefoot on red-hot coals. We have the model and you're going to learn it."

Then almost in a whisper he said, "I want you to imagine failure. Picture the worst. Burnt black, sizzling flesh. Yours! Excruciating, agonizing pain like you can't imagine. There will be no medals given for failure. The real heroes will be those who step forward now and admit they can't, at least for tonight. Are you one of them?"

A couple of people raised their hands. Early dropouts.

"Come on," I said to myself, "just go with the crowd. There's safety in numbers."

Then came the moment of challenge.

In almost a whisper Tony said, "Now, imagine how you will feel if you can walk on those coals."

There was silence and a long pause.

"What will you feel like inside?" he said.

The thought produced a surge of power. I could be more than I ever imagined. I commanded myself to do it, no matter what. We listened to the instructions over and over, and a mixture of martial arts and other mental pictures were riveted into my brain.

The moment of truth came and the line started to form. More dropouts raised their hands. Tony congratulated them as I grabbed Paige's hand.

"Move to the back of the line," I said.

The line inched closer and closer, as one after another did exactly as they had been told, making it through.

Finally it was time for the person in front of me. I watched his every move, as he went through the ritual we'd just been taught. Then he seemed to vanish in front of me. "OK," I told myself, breathing deeply several times. "This is it."

I stepped up to the line, dusted my feet off several times on the damp grass in front of the coals. There were red embers glowing down a three-foot wide path for at least thirty feet. I focused on a light some two hundred yards in the distance.

"This is it," I told myself. "Go to that light, no matter what."

I gritted my teeth and stepped quickly onto the coals. There was a crunch under my foot. Then another crunch. Surprisingly it felt like potato chips, but there was no heat. Then the sound of the next few steps. Crunch, crunch, crunch. One more crunch.

I wiped my feet on the wet ground; my fist shot up into the air.

"Yes," I shouted. I was amazed. I could somehow feel a shift, as if my brain had been re-wired.

The rest of the weekend was anticlimactic to the firewalk. Tony had baptized us in this way, so that we would see that results are a matter of modeled behavior, no matter how strange it seems to the mind. NLP demonstrates how to reprogram internal circuits, and I learned how to override fears with memories of empowerment. It was one more tool in my tool chest, although I wasn't confident yet.

"None of us will ever accomplish anything excellent or commanding except when he listens to this whisper which is heard by him alone."

Ralph Waldo Emerson

ON TO TALIESIN

It was my time. I felt compelled. Firewalking had ignited a sense of courage. Arriving at the office early, I nervously called Taliesin, Frank Lloyd Wright's estate. I wanted to find out if Wright had designed any collection or subdivision, but a cold call of any kind was one of my great fears. After I met someone, I could be comfortable and confident, skills I needed in the advertising business. But the cold call was a monster. My voice would crack and my throat would dry. I was patched through to Bruce Pfeiffer, the archivist. Cordially, yet nervously, I asked if Wright had ever planned a subdivision, not really wanting to blurt out what I had in mind. He said that a subdivision of low cost designs had been planned for South Carolina but never realized.

"Good," I thought. "It's still possible."

The land I had in mind was a magical 450-acre parcel on the island of Hawaii. Three volcanoes formed the backdrop, and the ocean spread out in the distance. The land was a sea of undulating rocky hills cut by streambeds and dotted by fountain grass that waved in unison under the almost constant trade winds. This was the sunny lee side of the island. At 600 to 1800 feet above sea level, there were warm days, exquisite sunsets over the water, and cool nights year round. While the distances appeared great, it was more of an optical illusion as resorts, beaches, and small communities were a short drive away. The wide variety of topographical features would complement Wright's designs.

Signal Oil owned the parcel. It had been on the market, yet large land tracts were not selling in 1984, and I had an "in" with Signal. They owned Kona Village Resort, and the resort was our advertising client. Bob McIntosh, Signal's representative, would be supportive, I told myself. We could work something out.

Randolph Galt, a grandson of the founder of Signal Oil, presently lived in Honolulu. Ran had been married to Anne Baxter, the movie star. The thread of synchronicity here formed a tight weave. Anne was also Frank Lloyd Wright's granddaughter. These relationships had to be signs that exceeded coincidence. I called Ran and spent an evening with him, laying out the gist of what I wanted to do. He wished me good luck.

Another confirming thread seemed to be the location of the land itself. From the time of King Kamehameha, the island lands were divided into pie-shaped configurations running from mountaintop to sea level, called "ahupua'a." Each ahupua'a was a self-contained unit offering climate suitable for agriculture, raising animals, and fishing.

The name of the ahupua'a containing the tract was called "Ouli, Place of Destiny." It included the "heiau", Pu'ukohola. Heiau were places of sacred power and worship. They usually had a temple platform including sacred buildings and symbolic images of the various gods. This heiau, one of the largest in all of Hawaii, had been built by King Kamehameha to honor the war god, Ku. It was from here that Kamehameha launched his successful effort to unite the Hawaiian Islands.

All of these elements seemed more than coincidence, as if destiny was at work, and I had my role to play.

Yet I still resisted. The echo of my astrology chart reverberated in me. I was not a loner, and never had been. My earliest memories were of my sandbox, and how Patti Pound, my three-year-old neighbor, would be brought over to play. We were two small children fully engaged in the most important things in our life — having fun in this sandbox by building castles and animals. Whatever I do in life, I want companions. I wanted a team of playmates. It would be more fun.

One of the folks in my agency knew of Kim Thompson, an architect who had studied at Taliesin.

I called Kim and we met at his office the next day. He was immediately likable, like a grown teddy bear. His office was strewn with books and papers, and Frank Lloyd Wright volumes sat beckoning to me behind his desk. There was an innocent craziness about him that immediately made me relax. He pulled out some designs and said, "I know these will work if the topography is like I think it is." His enthusiasm was infectious, as he seemed to know which unbuilt designs would fit.

At lunch I poured out my idea in more detail. His eyes lit up as we talked, and I told him about Rick Schulze and Charlie Campbell, my other two partners.

Impulsively I leaned over and said, "Kim, want to get into this with us?"

He grinned. "Yeah, Sandy, count me in."

He had been an apprentice, was married at Taliesin, and had lived there, at Taliesin West, the home of the Frank Lloyd Wright Fellowship. I sensed Kim wanted to return and reconnect at some level.

We formed the Waimea Development Group. The name emerged from the fact that Waimea, on the Big Island, was both the project's intended location and the home of my partners. The island has two-thirds of the world's climates. Waimea can seem like summer in Scotland. Brisk trade winds come off of the northwest, rise above Waipio Valley and shoot down this saddle. The sun is extremely bright. You feel nature's intensity there, like few places in Hawaii. Big sprawling country from mountain to ocean. The project land lay on the sunny side of Waimea, a few miles above the pristine beaches of Hapuna and Mauna Kea.

Charlie and I had met when his wife, Barbara, had selected my ad agency to handle the Kona Village Resort ad account. Behind his blond, boyish, ruddy New England complexion, there was some type of secret machine that radiated only well-being. When I met Charlie, it was as if our inner children decided to wrestle each other to the ground after having been apart for eons. Charlie seemed to have this kind of connection with everybody. He certainly had it with Bob McIntosh, Signal Oil's man in Hawaii. Bob and Charlie were constant fishing partners who would work something out around the land when the time came.

The final member of our band, Rick, was our spiritual warrior, and the one who would somehow keep us out of harm's way. When he spoke, we listened. He had been the "Note Editor" of the *Harvard Law Review*, the managing partner of one of the largest law firms in the state, the designer of the state reapportionment plan, and a federal district judge. He was asked to run for the United States Senate by the Democratic Party and to run for Lt. Governor by the Republican Party. At that time he was in his early thirties.

Somehow his spirit sent him on a course of self-discovery. He abandoned the life of fame and fortune to become a "country lawyer," marry a flower child, attend music school, and travel the world.

Rick had promised himself no more complicated legal endeavors, and no projects that would use up endless amounts of precious time. "But this I must admit..." He didn't need to say more. I knew.

Kim was excited; that excited me. And he had insights. He was a kindred soul, at least had been. He knew the inner sanctum of the Fellowship at Taliesin. It was the Fellowship that would accept or reject us. Even before I had met Kim, I sensed Taliesin to be a special place.

I wondered how we could approach them. We had no money and no development experience between the four of us.

The formal structure of the Frank Lloyd Wright Foundation was made up of an architectural school, the archives, and the Taliesin Associated Architects, which comprised an ongoing practice dedicated to carrying out Wright's philosophy of "Organic Architecture." They were the only ones empowered to build Wright's designs, and several of the architects there had been apprentices to him.

It was the Fellowship, however, that would vote on the matter. The Taliesin Fellowship was made up of the apprentices and members who had been accepted into the "family" by Mr. and Mrs. Wright, and only by Mrs. Wright after Wright's death in 1959. In some respects, the Fellowship was a commune with architecture as its focal point. Frank Lloyd Wright had called architecture the highest form of art, and here was a community drawn together to live life as an expression of art. The real influence for this idea had come from Olgivanna Wright. She had been a student of Russian philosopher G.I. Gurdjieff's for seven years at the Fontainebleau Institute in Paris. Gurdjieff's guiding principle had been an idea called the "Fourth Way." He felt that humanity was asleep, and life needed to be lived knowing that, as divine spiritual beings, our needs would be met by embracing to the fullest in faith and knowledge that the future would work out. The Fellowship thus had become a large extended family, living communally, and enjoying life lived as art. Since its beginnings, the Fellowship had expanded so that outsiders worked alongside the members. There was also Taliesin East in Spring Green, Wisconsin. In the summer months the family lived there, returning to Arizona for the winter. Though Frank Lloyd Wright had never been to Hawaii, he had designed an island home for Hilo Judge Martin Pence in the early '40s. Pence abandoned the idea when the estimates came in at double his budget.

60

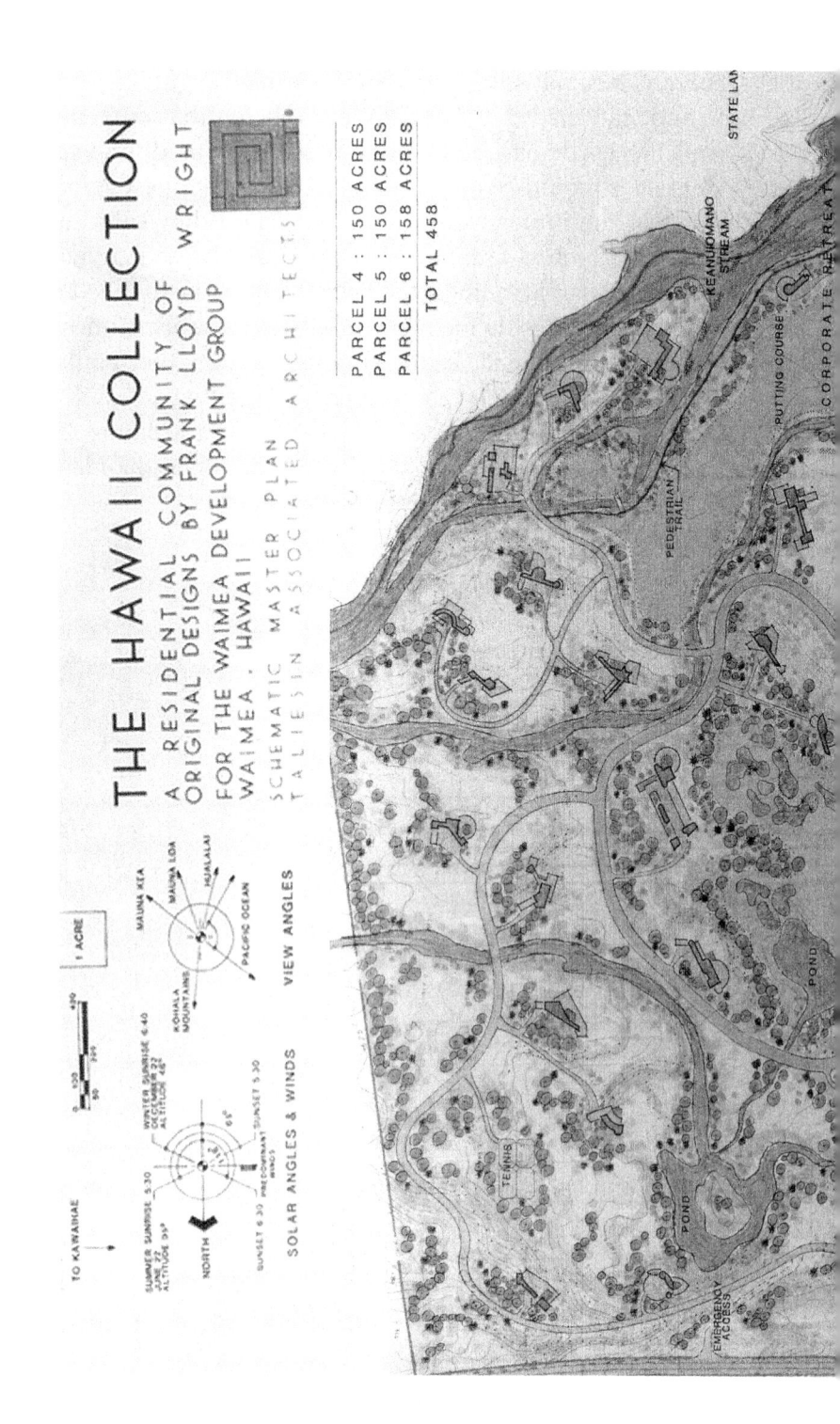

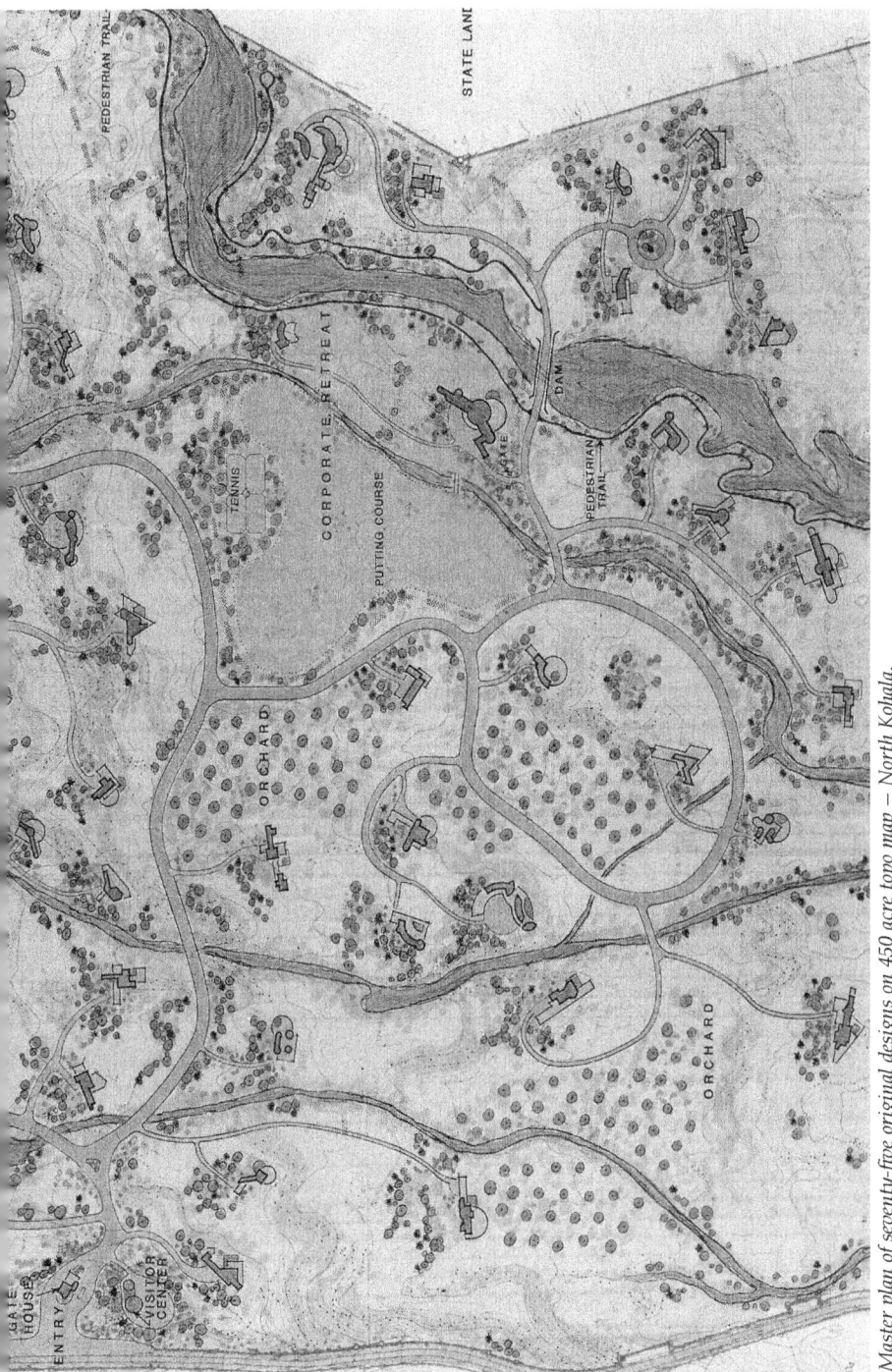

Master plan of seventy-five original designs on 450 acre topo map – North Kohala.

*"Follow your bliss.
Find where it is, and
don't be afraid to follow it."*

Joseph Campbell

The Die Is Cast

Kim called with good news.

"We're on for a presentation at Taliesin," he said.

I hung up. All kinds of emotions were at flood stage; relief, elation and fear. Relief that Kim had set up the appointment. Elation that we had an appointment, and fear that I had now stepped into the breach. No turning back.

It was "Proposal Time," and Kim had assembled a list of unbuilt designs he knew could work. As an ad man, proposals were second nature, but the inevitable challenge of "how to make a statement" gnawed at me. We had a simple idea; nothing else. No money, no knowledge, no development experience. Just an idea. How could we make ourselves special enough?

I woke up early with a simple idea: typeset the proposal!

A typeset proposal would jump off the page, in contrast to a normally typewritten proposal. In fact, I had never seen a typeset proposal. Artists would appreciate it; I was counting on that. There was unspoken support from agency staff members close to me. They sensed I was a Parsifal about to embark on the Hero's journey. The manuscript was read and reread, and then went to the typesetter and printer for a very short print run. Ten copies.

Three days later the package arrived. I tore off the wrapping. There it was, a plain, tan colored proposal to Taliesin for the "Hawaii Collection."

Rick, Kim and I left for Arizona, an architect, an ad guy and an attorney. In the end it would be about chemistry. They would either like us or not.

The plane drifted down through a cloud of brownish haze. Rooftops dotted the landscape in some random order, as if they had metastasized in all directions amidst an occasional mountain peak.

We settled into the McCormick Ranch, a resort not far from Taliesin in the heart of Scottsdale. From the air, everything seemed dusty and desert-like. But here there was green grass, and ponds and lakes. Scottsdale was a prosperous oasis, with large homes, wide avenues, new cars and glitzy stores.

The next morning Rick greeted the day with Sun Salutations and other yoga poses. I awakened slowly, watching Rick and vowing to myself that someday I'd do that too.

I wasn't hungry. I never am before presentations. The drive took us to the outskirts of Scottsdale, where the houses were less dense as we drove down Cactus Boulevard past stables, empty lots and ranchette structures. The road began to wind, up past the saguaro cactus plants. Then houses were gone. In the distance was the Cherokee red gate. A large monolithic rock stood there, and immediately I thought of the shamanic world, where a symbol of the upper world of teachers was often depicted by a tall standing rock obelisk.

The low horizontal line of the Taliesin West structure began to emerge, and the architectural design overshadowed the weathered look of the buildings. Kim told us that students had built the whole place under Wright's guidance. The massive rock walls and building faces were constructed using plywood forms. On the site, rocks and sand were mixed with cement, then poured into the forms. When dry, the forms were elevated, and the next layer added. This was called "Desert masonry." Every structure radiated a sense of community. Along the walkway, I gazed up to see a metal dragon shooting flames from its mouth: all part of the mystique.

We entered the large spacious drafting room. Natural light poured in from the slanted opaque ceilings, providing a warm glow. At the far end of the Cherokee red cement floors, a large fireplace gave the room a sense of both openness and intimacy. John Rattenbury, deep in concentration, caught a glimpse of us from the corner of his eye. "Kim," he said, "Great to see you!"

John was warm and radiated infectious enthusiasm. I felt an easiness as we chatted casually while touring the facilities. Taliesin West sits on 600 acres, nestled against mountains. John led the way to Frank Lloyd Wright's apartment. A tiny, almost disguised entrance squeezed us through a short narrow passage. Suddenly, we emerged into a spacious and inviting room. Opaque ceilings let light wash the room and there was a large off-center fireplace, built-in furniture, and chairs with sheepskin throws. The dining nook, with garden views, also held an immense fireplace that could burn logs standing on end. There was no wasted space; it was a jewel. What else would one expect of the Master's quarters? I pinched myself. Only a cosmic moment before I had been reading his autobiography. Now I was in his home!

The adjacent residential Fellowship apartments were all low-rise, made in the desert masonry style. We entered the cave-like cabaret theatre. Small glowworm lights strung across the ceiling made me feel secure, and comfortable. The next stop was a larger theatre, decorated in red tones, that revealed an ingenious way of changing sets for the stage. I saw the merging of art and life in this unique environment.

A few hundred yards away, various student structures dotted the desert. Each student had designed and built his own shelter. Some were quite elaborate, and they all were captivating.

"We teach by doing," John explained. "We wanted to be hands on from the beginning and let them encounter the practical side of building. Learn to make things and make them work. That in the end creates a good architect, maybe a great one."

The student shelters were for sleeping, studying and reflecting. Fireplaces provided heat in the cold desert nights, while the showers and lockers were in a larger facility. "It's a rich experience," John said. "In the morning, we might be repairing a roof, having classes, or doing chores. Saturday nights are often formal; tuxedos and evening dresses. Taliesin has been like a magical vortex. You could have been pouring cement earlier on in the day and mingling with luminaries, movie stars, statesmen, and diplomats in the evening. The list has been endless. People like Buckminster Fuller, Peter Ustinov, Georgia O'Keefe and

Ayn Rand have all come through."

We followed John though the large red double doors into the kitchen. Off to the left were big freezers, commercial ranges, and a prep area. Students and staff were serving lunch. We picked up plates and utensils and served ourselves. The dining room, warm and cozy with its low ceiling and a wall of glass, faced the outside breezeway. Midway Garden red metal chairs designed by Wright added color. There was a real sense of family, and everyone took turns working in the kitchen and dining room, regardless of age. They were a tribe on a wonderful journey together.

I turned to Kim. "Where do you think we're going to present?" He nodded. "John says we'll be going down to Bruce Pfeiffer's home."

Bruce, the archivist for the Foundation, we hadn't yet encountered, but I remembered our conversation. A casual walk took us down a gravel road away from the main buildings. In the distance, nestled amidst the saguaro cactus and other desert brush was a structure made up of intersecting circles. A jackrabbit darted in front of us. I hoped it would bring us luck.

We entered a small breezeway and then the Wright house. Off to the left was a small circular kitchen that Wright had referred to as a "workspace." Immediately I found myself in a circular room with green carpeting, built-in bench seating around the walls, hassocks, small tables and a large hearth. Several members of the Fellowship had come to hear our pitch. Among them Dick Casey, the administrative head, and Wes Peters, Wright's first apprentice, who was married for a short period of time to Joseph Stalin's daughter. I couldn't get my mind off of that fact. One of recent history's great tyrants and his DNA had briefly resided here. Then there was John, perhaps Taliesin's most prolific architect.

We sat in a circle. It's a nurturing way to meet: a sense of equality permeated the room. I told the story of how the idea came about, and how we had felt compelled to act.

I explained that we felt the synergistic value of a "collection" would be greater than the value of one of Wright's designs standing alone. In this regard we felt...

"Do you have any money?" someone asked.

"No," I said. "Just seed money to help us find the next partners."

Another voice: "Do you have land?"

"Yes," I said, "we have land." I explained our connection to the Signal land, knowing that we could work out a suitable arrangement with Bob McIntosh.

Afterward, there was the usual cordiality.

I heard Bruce exclaim to someone close by, "The proposal is typeset with today's date!"

He had noticed.

"We'll meet now," someone said, "and let you know tomorrow."

I felt if it was meant to be, so be it. If they refused the idea would be dead. If they accepted then our journey would have just begun. On the drive back to McCormick Ranch, we all speculated on outcomes.

The next day we drove out for our second meeting. It was a strange feeling, kind of an alchemy of calmness and anxiety. We sat down silently in one of the small presentation rooms. John said, "The Foundation has decided to give you the license."

"The fact that you have no money," John said, "is actually not a drawback. Money and good ideas rarely ever come in the same package."

Unknown to us was Frank Lloyd's Wright's philosophy about ideas. "The idea," he said, "was everything."

"You were willing to act on the idea with little else. That was a plus," John added.

We were floating.

Rick and their attorneys drew up the licensing arrangement. We had four years to make something happen. It was 1984, but certainly not Orwellian, and one leg of the journey was over. Now the real work would begin. What we didn't know was that Mrs. Wright had put a twenty-five year moratorium on Wright's designs upon his death in 1959, and we had arrived shortly after that moratorium had been lifted.

While the Frank Lloyd Wright Conservancy was dedicated to preservation, the Frank Lloyd Wright Fellowship was interested in promoting Wright's philosophy of organic architecture. So even though he was dead, the building of his designs with the latest materials, subject to local codes, would perpetuate his philosophy. Mrs. Wright agreed, and the designs were now available.

This was synchronicity: Kim's opening of the doors, and Mrs. Wright's lifting of the moratorium, just before we arrived. It seemed more than coincidental.

"The thing always happens you believe in, and the belief in a thing makes it happen."

Frank Lloyd Wright

LAND

Part two of the project was to secure the land. Signal owned 450 acres, but the real estate market had been very slow, with large parcels languishing. The total asking price for the 450 acres was $1.9 million.

Charlie and I made an appointment to see Bob McIntosh at Signal's headquarters in California. Things were moving quickly now, and the following week we were on a plane to California. When we arrived at the Western Airlines check-in at Honolulu, the ticketing agent said, "I see you're heading to Los Angeles. We'd like to give you a complimentary upgrade to first class." I looked at Charlie, and he winked; the Universe was with us.

Two hours into the flight there was an announcement, "Please get out your paper and pens for our halfway point contest. The entry closest to the actual distance will receive a bottle of champagne." Charlie laughed and said, "Get out your yellow pad."

He was reminding me of our trip to Australia years before, when we labored for days, trying to figure out how "gentlemen orchard growers" made money growing macadamia nuts. The yellow pads were littered with hopeless calculations, and usually the tax shelter idea would be a prominent decoy. One afternoon, in the back seat of the car somewhere near Milanda in Northern Australia I yelled, "Charlie I got it. The money isn't in nuts. It's in the small trees sold as starters."

I scratched away at the yellow pad, but nothing seemed to emerge. Reluctantly, I gave the attendant my number. She smiled and Charlie said, "Give me his number. Use these instead." She laughed. A half an hour later the announcement came. "Ladies and gentlemen we are happy to announce an unusual event. There are two winners. Two bottles of champagne. Dr. Charles Campbell and Sanderson Sims both bracketed the actual number.

We high-fived each other. Things felt good.

Signal's office was in Torrey Pines, a beautiful coastal California community. Charlie and Bob were longtime marlin-fishing buddies, and had fished the Kona Billfish Tournament together often. Bob, as the Signal representative at Kona Village Resort, was a client. It was a meeting of friends. I explained to Bob the Taliesin meeting I had just come from, and he was both intrigued and supportive. He saw our need to show control of the land.

"Look," he said, "Here's what I can do. Since nothing much is happening, I'll give you the first right of refusal on an option. Loose translation: if anybody else serious shows up, I'll let you know. Here are some topography maps." What a gift! John would need these to master plan the site.

That evening we were Bob's dinner guests. We talked about some of the work the agency was doing for Kona Village, fishing, and what Bob could do to assist us. The evening was delightful, as I thought about how the universe was supporting this idea.

Back in Honolulu, I got hold of John by phone. "We have the land and good news: I'm sending you topo maps today."

"Great Sandy. I'll have something for you to look at in four to six weeks."

John and I had previously discussed the strategy of using the land in incremental phases. There would be a first phase of twenty-five homes on 150 acres. The master plan would place homes on the appropriate building sites for each structure, based on topography contours. Some homes might be clustered. However, the density would average one home per five acres, with space around each building site falling into common areas. We planned to build homes averaging 3,000 square feet. There would be a visitor center, and parking. Homeowners would be required to allow tours of the home exterior, as is the practice at the Frank Lloyd Wright Home and Studio Foundation in Oak Park, Illinois. For part of the year, we would ask owners to occasionally open their homes. The first bill from Taliesin came. Nervously, I started dipping into my small cash reserves. Yet I had a sense of positive energy. While John was working on researching the archives, Rick and I began the task of preparing numbers and a presentation book. John sent us a few home transparencies he liked, as well as plans for a focus home, the Hargrove house. Originally designed for California living, it would be the first to be constructed. People would see firsthand what an original Wright home built to code, using modern materials, looked like in Hawaii.

A large tube arrived by mail. I popped off the end and pulled out the large roll, sliding the bands off gently. I had a sense of reverence and awe, feeling that I was now part of a larger idea, not my own, but something bigger. Here were designs and instructions in Wright's own hand. The print was tiny, and exquisitely precise. It felt like a treasure map, and it was. The curves, windows, details and lines were enchanting.

Kim found an estimator. The number that came back, $650,000, was the first breath of reality. It felt good, though we were going to have to at least double that figure, and then hope that it would cover the costs.

The land for the focus home had been purchased earlier from Frank Clement. It was a gorgeous three-acre parcel on a small bluff distantly facing three volcanoes and the ocean. In the foreground, a seasonal stream branched to both sides of a small island. Three hundred thousand acres of pristine state-owned land stretched for as far as the eye could see.

We pulled off of the main highway outside of Bakersfield, California; the road carried us along acres of vineyards until we came to a large hacienda tucked in among fruit orchards. The driveway brought us to a U-shaped courtyard. A Madonna figure graced a fountain in the middle, and off to the right, in back of the house, was a huge tower, the largest ham radio tower in America. Charlie rang the buzzer. Standing before us was Frank, the archetypal mad scientist, tall and lean and white hair "frizzed" like hundreds of antennae.

"Charlie, great to have you here," he said.

Frank shook my hand, and beckoned us back to the kitchen.

Frank had been one of America's unofficial contacts with North Vietnam during the war, allowing prisoners to talk to their homes by ham radio. We spent hours around that breakfast table entranced by Frank, who made science come alive for us. "Here, let me show you what I plan to do on the small island," Frank said as he pointed to the topographical map he had produced. The seasonal stream, when running, flowed around a landmass, making it an island. Frank had a kit home all picked out. It was a raised structure, sitting on a large concrete cylinder. He wanted to make a swinging bridge over to the island where the home would be. I wondered to myself how he would ever get a building permit, since the island was in a flood plain.

Frank was a fire hydrant of ideas, pouring them out. I didn't understand half of what he said, but it didn't matter. He was tapping into some other place in the universe, and Charlie and I realized we were in the slipstream of a wizard. Then, as if in midstream, Frank slowed down.

"As much as I would like to do this, I have to face the fact that flying is out. My ears can't take the change in altitude." I sensed the disappointment in Frank's voice, yet I felt a surge of excitement, knowing that we could place our focus home here, and it would be stunning.

A few weeks later a large package arrived, containing the site master plan. I scurried over to Kim's office, and I carefully took the drawing out and laid it down. There in detail were seventy-five original designs of Frank Lloyd Wright's. All were drawn to scale on the topo maps. These were not just indications, but the actual exterior floor plan outlines for each design. John sited the homes not according to lot lines, but to how they should appear on the land. In some cases the homes were bunched together. In others they were free-standing on an isolated section. We would be asking the county for a planned unit development. Under that land designation owners would purchase the home site and then share an undivided interest in the remaining land.

We couldn't believe what we were looking at. These were treasures, the work of the Master. We could never have seen them during Wright's lifetime, because plans prepared for clients would have remained filed.

A new client would be given a new plan, and though old plans might have been the inspiration for a new client, they certainly would not have been the new client's plan. However, after Wright's death, these plans became the historical memoirs of a genius. The Hawaii Collection had moved to the next stage.

The plan showed three phases of twenty-five homes each. Some were large homes that could be used as corporate retreats. There was a visitor center in the first phase, and orchards, waterscapes, and neighborhood amenities were contoured to the land. John had gone all out to show what these 450 acres could look like. Whether or not the project would ever succeed, I knew that his effort was a remarkable accomplishment. If even a fraction of these homes could be built, the project would be magnificent.

*"The power of intuitive
understanding will protect you
from harm until the end of your days."*

Lao Tzu

CAUGHT BETWEEN TWO BELIEF SYSTEMS

Now the laborious task began of making projections about sales, costs, cash flow, and all the areas where we had no experience. Slowly projections and time-frames began to emerge. I became immersed in the deadly seduction of believing that the numbers we were preparing represented reality. We took the estimate for the focus home and doubled the cost. Though our infrastructure numbers were a best guess, based on conversations with developers, it wasn't as if we had made up the numbers. However, even the best estimates were only that.

I didn't have the $1.9 million needed to purchase the land, but I didn't want to see it slip away. There had been enough orientation through my experience with the Findhorn community to want to believe that if my desires were on purpose, and not fear-based, I could commit and move forward. I wouldn't know where the funds would come from, only that they would come.

The statement attributed to Goethe by the Scotsman, W.H. Murray, haunted me:

"Until one is committed, there is hesitancy, the chance to draw back. Concerning all acts of initiative (and creation), there is one elementary truth, the ignorance of which kills countless ideas and splendid plans: that the moment one definitely commits oneself, then Providence moves, too. All sorts of things occur to help one that would never otherwise have occurred. A whole stream of events issues from the decision, raising in one's favor all manner of unforeseen incidents and meetings and material assistance, which no man could have dreamed would have come his way. Whatever you can do, or dream you can do, begin it. Boldness has genius, power, and magic in it. Begin it now."

If I lacked the courage to make the commitment, all would be lost. The land would be sold to someone else, and the project would collapse. If I did make a commitment to purchase, and I could not, then I would lose much, if not all, of what I had worked so many years to create. I was afraid and confused. I thought of how hard I had worked. Yes, perhaps, I could get it all together again if I failed, but would I have the energy? Would I be finished?

After a night of cold sweat, I decided that if I were truly committed, Providence would come to my aid. It was then that I finally decided. I resolved to make the offer. I had finally come to believe that forces would conspire to aid me, that I did have "Invisible Partners" who would organize the unfolding of a magical path. Some kind of guiding hands were nudging me forward. It was these Invisible Partners that I felt as the energy to go forward, and the signposts along the way that kept me from going crazy.

I asked myself what my motives were. Was I on an ego trip? Was I hoping to make a lot of money to extinguish my insecurity, my lack of faith in my own creative power, the power I had been awakened to? Or was this really a great adventure?

I decided that strong intuitive hits or hunches or guidance were my links to a larger reality, and to make it more "down to earth" I wanted to think that I had associates, brighter and more visionary, more conscious, who needed me as much as I needed them. The words of Hermes Trismegistus in the *Emerald Tablet*, "As above so below," reverberated in me. I found comfort in accepting the idea that God perhaps was an unfathomable intelligence and energy that manifested and revealed itself in ever-expanding forms of consciousness that we embrace and embody through an infinite journey. I could only imagine just so far, and then no further. But did it really matter? At least from this point of view, everything I thought of was a lesser consciousness, no matter how grand it was. My Invisible Partners would have the idea and direction, but would need hands, feet and a mind to operate in this reality, and that was the partnership for the adventure. And as far as free will went, if I had the energy as well as the desire to have a pure experience, not out of fear, but just to have it, then these same partners would respond to help me. My response seemed entirely up to me, but while it was resolved in my mind, it was not resolved emotionally. I was still afraid, but willing to move forward.

That morning in the office I picked up the phone and dialed the law office. The rings seemed eternal before the connection.

"Rick," I said, "I'm ready." There was a long silence. He knew my state exactly. The famous "falling" dream, which I had had many times, came to mind. Each time, careening toward Earth and certain death, I woke up in a panic. One night in the dream I said, "Screw it." Instead of passing headlong into the unknown, my body began to slow down as the ground approached. A gentle force slowed me down and placed me on a beautiful white sand beach. I had gone through the fear in my dream to survive in this most benign fashion. Remembering this, I said to Rick, "Let's do it. Make the offer."

A few days later, the final purchase contract Rick had negotiated for me was ready to sign. In fourteen short months, $1.9 million would be due. It would be my complete undoing if I failed. The next morning we were to meet in his office and launch my appointment with destiny.

Rick called that evening. "Sandy," he said, "I'm not going to let you do it. I'm simply not going to let you. I'm going to save you from yourself. We're not signing any contract."

Our deal was not bound by location. Land ownership was paradoxical. We needed to show we had land and how the idea could come alive there. Yet having land meant being tied down. I felt a huge relief, as if I had passed an initiation. But this was countered by a sense of emptiness, a vacuum, as the land acquisition would have shown solidity. There had been so many synchronicities around the land. Was I indeed abandoning the path? Would this idea now simply end in some backwater tide pool, rather than catching the wave of a glorious ride, or was this some divine hand opening up opportunities we couldn't see? We had no experience in development, and were asking for an investor to finance our education.

Rick and I then set about to make the presentation as strong as possible. Our numbers, we were later to find out, were not that bad. Nobody really knew what Frank Lloyd Wright original designs would cost. Costs per square foot are usually based upon experiences that average out, but these designs would be in a new paradigm. Infrastructure figures were also iffy. Roads, water, utilities, the permit process, availability of workers, and many unknowns, could all be problems.

*"There is a tide in the affairs of men,
which, taken at the flood, leads on to fortune;
Omitted, all the voyage of their life
is bound in shallows and in miseries."*

***Shakespeare, Julius Caesar* IV, iii**

The Hero's Journey Begins

Reverberating through me were Joseph Campbell's many metaphors about hearing the call and venturing out into the unknown naked and naïve. Until now, everything had been preparation for the big step: finding financial backing. While the land issue had disappeared, there was a new specter to haunt me: vagueness. At least with land and a license we felt more grounded.

My first targets were organizations that had successfully financed development in Hawaii, like insurance companies. In this case we would be the developers, and they would provide the backing. Wealthy individuals interested in the Arts were another market. The large auction houses, Sotheby's and Christie's, might direct us to potential sources, for Sotheby's had a real estate division. Finally, and probably the most promising, would be to find a developer who saw this idea as worth doing.

I hated "cold calls" over the phone, but I had to begin. I didn't know what else to do. It was like being in becalmed waters in the middle of the ocean. I had no wind, but I had oars. If I did nothing, I would go nowhere. If I started rowing at least I was making an effort. Yet, there was something rude about barging unannounced into someone's life, forcing the unsuspecting listener to drop what they were doing to hear me. What a helpless and foolish feeling it created in me, and some days I dreaded it. Yet I pushed on.

The project was infinitely fascinating to me, but most people did not have time, or felt it would be too much, coming out of the blue from a stranger with no introductions or references. For many it was such a strange call that they were intrigued enough to listen to me and wish me well.

I wrote letters to very wealthy people, many of whom returned short notes cheering me on. But there was no personal interest. I knew no other way, but I had to keep the energy flowing.

Finally I felt it was time to up the ante. I'd have to put myself out there, get on the road, and go face-to-face. My first destination was Sotheby's in New York. The connection of art and real estate felt like the first right step, and this act seemed to gather support in ways I couldn't understand.

Kyle Rote, the famous football player, and his wife, Nina, became supporters. They took me under their wing and gave me encouragement. People everywhere were curious and courteous, and genuinely intrigued.

The next stop was Lincoln, Nebraska, to visit with the insurance company representatives who financed Chris Hemmeter's Hyatt Hotel in Waikiki. People were cheering me on, but the project seemed too far away, too abstract for serious money-makers. Maybe I was seen as more of a messenger than someone to be trusted with such a large project. With no development track record, who would give me large sums of money? In my hotel room, I felt worn, but I never doubted that good would come from the effort. There was an energetic force propelling me along, and though I was jousting with windmills, I wasn't discouraged.

Returning to Honolulu, I kept at it for what seemed forever. Then one day there was a call from Tonia Baney, of the Wailea Development Company on Maui. It was a big agency client, and she was the marketing director. She had grown up just a few miles from Taliesin East in Spring Green, Wisconsin and was a big fan of Frank Lloyd Wright, and a big supporter of me in this project.

"Sandy" she said, "I have a couple of gentlemen who are interested in taking you to lunch. They like your idea. Have fun, and call me."

The small café was bright and cheerful, a good sign. At a small table were two local Japanese gentlemen. Pundy Yokouchi, often referred to as "Mr. Maui," a major political power broker on the island, was a graceful, soft-spoken man in his late sixties. He had started as a baker and had become involved in one successful venture after another, many in real estate. Seated beside him was Howard Hammamoto, a recently retired top executive from American Factors, one of Hawaii's "Big Five" companies.

Pundy got right to the point.

"Sandy, we've heard about your Frank Lloyd Wright idea. It has just what we need for our Maui development." They briefly mentioned their third partner, Takeschi Sekiguchi, who had become known as a miracle worker, turning virtually every Japanese real estate investment in Hawaii into pure gold. He was then building the Four Seasons and Grand Wailea hotels on Maui. Sekiguchi, it was rumored, could commit up to $200,000,000 with the stroke of his pen. Their partnership, Waikapu Mauka Partners, had acquired 600 acres on the slopes of the West Maui Mountains. The land was agriculturally zoned, and Brewer, a large landowner, had seen no real potential in it. For Pundy's group, it was an entirely different matter. They had an idea, and the money to carry it out.

Howard and Pundy outlined their plan: build two adjacent golf courses, one private and very exclusive. For the exclusive course, offer private memberships to wealthy Japanese for $250,000 each. The Japanese economy was going wild, riding an economic tsunami wave. The Japanese were gobbling up trophy real estate around the world, and the wealth creation was staggering. In downtown Tokyo a single parking space was rumored to be selling for as much as a $1 million. The Japanese love affair with Hawaii was eternal, as was their fascination and admiration with Frank Lloyd Wright's genius. The timing was perfect.

From anywhere on the exclusive golf course, there would be breath-taking views of the ocean on both sides of the island simultaneously. Two hundred exclusive homes sites on two-acre lots would surround the course. Their hope was to turn Wright's home design for Marilyn Monroe into a clubhouse, and to have thirty of the 200 homes be original Wright designs. Frank Lloyd Wright was an icon in Japan. When the great Kanto earthquake of 1923 struck Tokyo, virtually leveling the city, the Imperial Hotel, designed by Wright, remained standing; not one pane of glass was broken. The Japanese were astonished, and he instantly became a legend. Marilyn Monroe held a similar fascination. Added to this alchemy was the Japanese craze at the time for everything western. Wright and Monroe converging in Hawaii, in their view, would be irresistible when offered in Japan. Sekiguchi had arranged for the financial backing of the Shimizu Corporation, a huge international construction firm. The Wright designs in this compound could easily be pre-sold in Japan, and the club memberships would be scooped up there.

Now, at last, the invisible veil was lifting. I could see the clubhouse and homes coming out of the ether, creating a magnificent artistic statement. Strangely I felt calm and even, rather than ecstatic. I didn't want to feel too hollow if all of this got derailed. I called Rick, Charlie and Kim after this memorable lunch. Our first real opportunity had arrived. If we could structure the right deal, professional developers would take over. We could concentrate on promotion and tourism once the houses were built. Had our Invisible Partners been busy? It appeared so.

"The reward of a thing well done is to have done it."

Ralph Waldo Emerson

BACK TO TALIESIN

The Waikapu Mauka Partners, Howard, Pundy, and Sekiguchi, along with members of the Shimizu Corporation, went to Taliesin, and Rick, Kim, and I met them there. Both Rick's wife, Susan, and my wife, Susanne, were young, vivacious and accompanying us to soften the energy.

We gained access to the off-limits archives and looked at the original plans of the Master. The Imperial Hotel, one of Tokyo's great landmarks, hand built from stone, was the first plan we saw. I heard one of the Japanese men from the Shimizu Corporation whisper to his friend, "We tore it down." Like many other great artistic and cultural landmarks, it had died from economic obsolescence.

Everything rode on Rick now. He had both a daunting and ticklish task. Our little group had to be granted a license by Taliesin. Simultaneously he had to negotiate a deal with the Waikapu Mauka Partners and Taliesin. Leaving both Taliesin and Pundy's group feeling good was a thankless position, and everyone knew it. The week was filled with Rick's elation and sweat, as he negotiated the best for Taliesin without killing the deal.

Finally, Waikapu Mauka Partners gained the right to build thirty original homes, plus a clubhouse which would expand the unrealized home design for Marilyn Monroe and Arthur Miller. A house design of 7,000 square feet would develop into a building of over 70,000 square feet; modified to include locker rooms, a spa and pro shop. The Shimizu organization would look to sell exclusive golf memberships in Japan for $250,000 each to as many as 800 people. There would be up to 200 homes on two acres each with 30 of these homes being original Wright designs. These would be brought up to code, with state of the art materials and features.

One of the unresolved issues was conducting home tours while not jeopardizing the sale of these homes. Our group was to receive a percentage of the home sales, design fees, and rights to operate the home tours.

It seemed unreal to receive our initial payment of $200,000, but the idea was taking root, really happening. Taliesin was to receive a full 15 percent architectural fee on all of Wright's designs. We were elated. Rick had done a masterful job for both Taliesin and us. We started with nothing more than an idea, and now the money and know-how had arrived. We had come a long way.

Work on the clubhouse was to commence immediately, costing about $30 million. Eventually, some $4.5 million would find its way into the Foundation's sorely deficient coffers.

The Foundation had presently stalled, wading into the development world with an exclusive housing project called Taliesin Gates adjacent to Taliesin West. They had made substantial investments in roads, water and power, as well as the building of a focus home; it all had created a serious cash strain. They sold prized art to pay bills and the arrival of this fee, like manna from heaven, removed a good deal of the debt issues. The Fellowship's collective Invisible Partners seemed to be on the job.

We had been tested, but the best of all outcomes was blossoming. None of our small group had had any development experience, but the willingness to persist and trust seemed to be magically paying off. One major developer had said to us in his office, "Are you guys trying to make any money?"

He sensed what we knew: we were on a grand adventure. The money was secondary, but we wanted to make some profit. But each of us wanted much more; we wanted to be stunned by the realization of this exquisite land art.

The Clubhouse on Maui. Courtesy Jim Cazel Photography

"Trust in dreams, for in them is hidden the gate to eternity."

Kahlil Gibran

THE PROJECT STARTS

The construction of two golf courses got underway. Taliesin moved extremely quickly under John's leadership, while Howard took charge of development and creating the marketing and sales materials. My advertising firm, Peck Sims Mueller, landed the graphics assignments. It turned out to be one of our most difficult ever. We needed to convey to the imagination what didn't exist. The final bill for 8,000 brochures alone came to $400,000. Staggering, yet consistent with the required image. Howard was pushing hard to bring the project to market, and get the memberships sold and the homes spoken for. He sensed that the sooner this process started the more likely it would be to succeed. Shimizu, on the other hand, was on a different schedule. They had no sense of urgency, and felt that each day that more was completed on the golf course and clubhouse made their project more real to prospects. The Shimizu people believed we were just entering Japan's Golden Age with no end in sight. Rumors were the Wright homes had already been spoken for in Japan.

Then in 1990, horror! The Japanese stock market crashed. The potential golf membership market vanished instantly, sweeping us away as if a huge tsunami had roared ashore. Internal realignments took place in the Shimizu organization, quickly sounding our death knell. On the side of the West Maui Mountains sat a magnificent clubhouse ready to be used, surrounded by an exquisite golf course ready for play, but there was now no market for expensive homes and certainly no market for $250,000 golf memberships. This show was over. It happened so fast, so utterly fast, like a severed limb preceding the pain. Years of work, and so close, so very close. I was numb, sad and disappointed, but not devastated. Maybe it was the Buddhist philosophy anesthetizing my emotions: feel no great sadness in loss, and no great joy in accomplishment.

While my dream faded, there was a sense of completion at another level, as if Buckminster's concept of "Precession" had come into full play: the idea that the true purpose of one's endeavor is occurring at 90 degrees to the direction of focus. The bumblebee is on a mission of gathering nectar, while unknowingly pollinating the landscape. Had we been doing the same thing? Had we simply appeared at a time when Taliesin needed a cash infusion? A visionary trip had swept us along, presenting incredible people and adding richness to our lives. We had not been penalized or really harmed in any way. It was as if the lights had come on at the end of the film. We sat watching the credits, reflecting on the movie, and getting ready to get up and go back to our other world. There was no strength for another shot, at least not now. I was at peace, and it was time for a rest.

"Look at every path closely and deliberately.
Try it as many times as you think is necessary.
Then ask yourself, and yourself alone, one question.
Does this path have a heart?
If it does, the path is good;
if it doesn't, it is of no use."

Carlos Castaneda

A Strange Thing Happens On The Way To The...

While looking for a joint partner, I had attended one of the Frank Lloyd Wright Conservancy meetings in Seattle, where owners of Wright's homes across America gathered once a year. Not immensely wealthy people, they were mostly an eclectic group of teachers, professionals, and people who enjoyed a passion for the arts. One of the speakers profoundly moved me when he said that we were not so much homeowners as stewards of these timeless designs.

My focus shifted as I remembered attending a Jean Houston seminar in Honolulu. Jean, one of the founders of the Human Potential Movement, talked about being able to access the essence of a discipline. In the course of the session, she had us standing and moving our bodies as if our gyrations were not connected to rational thought. We were altering and bypassing the gatekeepers of our normal thinking circuitry. To demonstrate, she asked if anyone in the audience played the piano. A hand went up not too far from her. A pleasant man smiled. She beckoned him to the stage, and asked him what style of piano training he had had. Bewildered, he blurted out his piano teacher's name to light laughter from the audience. Jean asked that we, as well as this gentleman, engage in the exercises for a few minutes. He, however, was also instructed to intend to access the essence of music. She asked him to bring back a written but unpublished Mozart piece, and the room again was a mass of flinging arms, disjointed hips, and wild contortions. Sure enough, within moments, our man sat down, with fingers racing across the keyboard. Out popped a Mozart composition. I thought to myself, "I know some Mozart, but certainly not enough to recognize what's never been published." For an encore he was instructed to bring back an unpublished show tune from Rodgers and Hammerstein. She had my attention now. Sure enough he played a tune. "A 'shill?'" I wondered. Then I quickly dismissed that idea on the basis of the damage it would do to her career if it were revealed.

Wright apparently designed using this gift. Now more than ever, I was fascinated by the energy patterns of a design coming from those realms. What would it be like to reside inside the pattern, inside the hologram?

What would I feel? Would it change the way I thought? What else might happen? The idea germinated, slowly sprouting, becoming more and more intriguing. I began to study sacred geometry and related topics such as the Fibonacci series. These disciplines explain the order and harmonic relationships of patterns occurring in nature. Wright had said that architecture is the highest form of art, but what is art?

So far, at least for me, the best explanation had come from James Joyce in his *Portrait of An Artist*. He said that there were essentially two kinds of art. The first is kinetic art, or that which promotes movement. Rock and roll music would be a good example. The other and highest form Joyce called static: this art arrests, puts the beholder in a state of awe, of non-thinking, receptive, profound appreciation. It transcends all intellectual constrictions. A cave man and a New York art critic might both drop their jaws at a multicolored sunset. Profound states seem to be a portal to grace and the appreciation for the miracle of the present moment. Meditation's goal has the same effect; to still the mind and reach a space of receptivity.

I had always pondered the suggestion that truth, beauty and goodness were one in the same. As Terence McKenna had said, "It seems to me very difficult to know what is really true and good, but much easier to realize what is beautiful." As a result, seeking beauty became my new goal, and I felt like that would be reward enough. Since architecture was the highest form of art for Frank Lloyd Wright, I wondered if by living inside one of his designs truth and goodness might reveal themselves to me.

By the time the venture on Maui was over, the acres set aside by Signal had been sold. The three-acre site, however, was still available, and beckoning. John's urging to build one of these homes in Hawaii stayed with me.

The building fever was slowly seducing me. John had selected the Hargrove house, originally designed for a California family. It was gorgeous, exquisite and enticing. The cost estimate might be a little higher than we previously figured, but probably I could afford it. All of the rationalizations were creating unbridled enthusiasm. It had happened so many times in life: these urges to seize an opportunity, to move now, not so much by thinking, but by feeling. I wondered if my Invisible Partners were just putting on the pressure. I have wrestled with the idea that not only do we order forces into play with our intentions, but are equally partnered with other forces that emanate from a consciousness outside of our own. When we are the recipient of an urge or intuition, where is this urge coming from? Whose Ideas are these? It was too much for me to comprehend that some omnipresent force was at work in everybody's lives all of the time, but easier to feel that I had a group of buddies in the invisible world, much closer at hand, and with greater vision. Together we were muddling through on joint projects, using my physical capabilities to manifest in the physical world. I liked this way of seeing things. It felt so orderly, manageable, and calming. I could quit trying to figure it all out and concentrate on savoring the journey and smoothing out the ride: that's what I wanted to do.

"As above so below," reverberated in me. Instead of leaps into divine hoopla, perhaps our lives and deaths are a much more ordered and gradual change between our physical world and the invisible world. Maybe all souls are on a grand, ever-expanding recycling journey, responding in kind to ever-increasing levels of consciousness. This was challenging enough for me. All around, I could sense us moving into an ever more complex world, with less and less time to figure it all out. We are, like it or not, having to tune into our intuition and give it more validity. Time to contemplate is vanishing. Perhaps we are being called on to trust these impulses, more so now than ever before. Our brains are becoming better at responding and reacting. The alternatives, resistance and non-acceptance, seem to lead to worry, despair, and physical disease. Our evolutionary journey has always been a survival of the fittest. For millions of years the struggle was to survive. Next came breakthroughs in using our brains to create in the physical world, measured in thousands of years. The challenge now was to learn how to trust while thinking, as a means of surviving in the physical world. To do so required expanding the muscles of consciousness, and conscious behavior. This journey, one could argue, had been measured in hundreds of years.

While perhaps these were the machinations of my Virgo mind, I scared up the courage to keep testing these waters.

I had $250,000 in my bank account. While the agency was going strong, and income projections looked healthy, debt was a devil I didn't want to dance with, nor did I want to leave some half-finished memorial. But I had been there before. If this house were meant to be, then the forces necessary to see it through would show up.

Unlike the vast majority of Frank Lloyd Wright's clients, we were partners with the Foundation. This was an extension of our business idea. If we built a home, it would become a seed, a Frank Lloyd Wright home in Hawaii, and could eventually spawn the Collection idea. The 450 acres of land below us, containing the master plan, was sold. It was too late for our idea to spring up there. Yet if the house went up who knew what could come from it? Our idea from the beginning was to build a sample home knowing we would eventually sell it.

John and his wife Kay returned to Hawaii and stopped by the site for some final inspections. As Kay reached to open the door, the wind caught it, almost ripping it from its hinges. Madam Pele, the fiery goddess of the volcanoes, was on a rampage. John turned to me and said, "I think we're going to need another plan." It was fortuitous. Had he not experienced this big blow, the house might have been built suitable for the terrain, but woefully inadequate for nature's predictability in this blustery saddle between two mountains.

John knew instantly which designs to consider: Frank Lloyd Wright had created a small series of hemicycle homes. Think of a design in the shape of a third of a donut. An earth berm covers the back of the first floor. Big gusts can slam into the berm and the back of the second floor, which is mostly cement block, and sail right over the flat roof. The lee of the house, composed of two stories of solid glass, remains totally calm.

When John learned that Susanne and I were visiting her family in Minneapolis, he encouraged us to call Don and Virginia Loveness, longtime friends of the Fellowship. They lived in Stillwater, a short drive away, and had constructed two Wright plans — the first literally built with their own hands, and later a small cottage.

Two of Frank Lloyd Wright's jewels appeared as we pulled into the forested drive. Don, a rugged barrel-chested fellow, strode out to meet us.

Virginia, a small but determined lady with an air of unbridled enthusiasm, welcomed us at the door. She was dressed in an original Issey Miyake outfit and it was no surprise to learn she had been a curator for New York's Metropolitan Museum of Art. Don, a chemist with 3M, was now retired.

"All of the fears tugged at me about approaching the great architect," Virginia said. "Especially since we had no money. I guess he was intrigued by our determination. We were sincere. Maybe he was rooting for us to succeed, but that initial winter was a bear. We were living on the site in a small trailer, building this first house brick by brick with our own hands."

"A pretty remarkable undertaking," I thought, as we marveled at the fieldstone and polished red floors. Here was the unmistakable distinct Wrightian energy that I had come to recognize. We followed a narrow path connecting the main house to the cottage where they now lived. I felt as if I had crossed an imaginary veil into a fairy tale setting. Set next to a pond was the most exquisite small structure I had ever seen. Sun rays shimmered through birchwoods, and a carpet of lawn ran to the water's edge. It was completely still, and I was not aware of another dwelling anywhere. Fairies could have appeared at any moment and I would not have been surprised.

From the side I saw a wall of glass with a high, sloping shed roof. I didn't see the front door at first, since it was part of the glass side. At the entrance, and to the immediate left, a two-story wall of glass ran the entire length of the cottage from ceiling to built-in cabinets. Beautiful *objets d'art* adorned the surface, and the waist-level view to the lake enchanted me. To the right was a small open workspace kitchen, shaped like a horseshoe; it too opened to the lake view. Straight ahead there was a long regal wooden dining table, and intricately carved highback chairs. From the seat at the head of the table I gazed to the lake, then turned to look at the huge fireplace, one large enough to roast a wild boar. It was a feast for the eyes. Above the dining table the high part of the shed roof gave me the feeling of being in a large banquet hall, though the roof slanted down, flattening out to create a cozy living space with built-in sofas. The patio, appearing through the glass as an extension of the living room area, could easily accommodate 50 or more people. I entered the bedroom through a small entrance next to the fireplace, a cave-like space with clerestory windows at shoulder height. A sliding door led to a tiny bathroom. Inside, a subtle sliding door opened. I climbed a miniature staircase to a secret loft. It had a small sofa and a sewing machine. You could see down, but nobody would expect you to be there. Some have said there was more architecture per square foot in the 1,000 square feet of this cottage than in any other structure in America. I wanted to move in and spend the rest of my life there.

We intended to spend an hour, but found ourselves enthralled, listening to many stories about the Fellowship and their adventures as pre-Columbian and oriental treasure hunters, especially about the alabaster Buddha head for which four people had lost their lives when bringing it out of Burma.

We told Don and Virginia about our project, which was well along.

"Call John. See if this plan is available," said Don, unfurling a set of floor plans. "It's a real treasure. We almost built it ourselves." It was called the Cornwell House, designed by Wright in 1954.

What caught our eyes was the alcove at the far end of the living area. Football shaped, with built-in seating along one side, it was the perfect configuration for seminars and small gatherings. The view to the right was through the prow-shaped two-storied mitered glass. Directly above was a bedroom, with shutters opening to the interior and the view out. Two intersecting overlapping circles made the football shape, referred to as a Vesica Pisces in sacred geometry. What made it even more enchanting was the view through the prow glass to the seasonal stream. When it raged, you almost felt the water would pour into the living room. Before we knew it, ten hours had slipped by as if we had been in a dream.

John said that the Cornwell house was available, and would work equally well. Two choices now tugged at me. John had selected the Martin house. I couldn't really interpret architectural plans, but trusted that our visit with Don had more of a purpose than just a visit. There was undeniable synchronicity, since Don's plan was in the same hemicycle family. We pored over the details, realizing they were meant to be. It was among the last of some 1,000 of Wright's plans, and I felt that it contained all of the wisdom his genius embodied. Developed in 1954 for this Pennsylvania family, it was not built by the Foundation. "I've got a good feeling about this, John," I called back to say, "Let's go with the Cornwell plans."

Our setting was perfect. The house, with its large overhangs, was a passive solar design. Facing south, the sun would ride low on the horizon in winter, sending penetrating rays through the two stories of glass to radiate off of the brick walls. In the summer, from high in the heavens, the sun's rays would be blocked by the large overhangs, thereby maintaining coolness. Since this house was situated at 1,800 feet, in a year-round tropical climate the temperature would be nearly perfect.

This two-story house in Hawaii would back up to the wind, and the protected all-glass front would inwardly wrap around the small semicircular lawn. Abruptly the yard would end with a sharp drop to a seasonal stream. The stream encircled a small island. The view from the front of the house would be across the island in the immediate foreground to a sprawling wide-open prairie of fountain grass. On some days, you could see the ocean and three volcanoes, perhaps covered with snow. The second floor echoed the same view. Since it was hanging from the ceiling by concealed steel rods, there was no need for interior support posts on the ground floor. The effect was to accomplish one of Wright's principles of organic architecture, the feeling that the indoors and outdoors blended and merged.

A series of ten-foot-high double doors formed the front of the house, opening to the outside circular walkway, the lawn and a magnificent view. At one end of the curve was a large cylinder. It rose through the second floor and contained a stairwell and two of the bathrooms above. Below, on the first floor of the cylinder, was another small half-bath and laundry room. The living room, or great room, spanned some 90 feet in an arc connecting the dining alcove to the alcove at the far end. Upstairs, the house had been designed to give privacy. The master suite was quite large, complete with fireplace, walk-in closet and outside porch. A large sky-lighted bathroom included two sinks, bath, bidet closet, and shower. There were two smaller rooms for the little boys, and at the far end a private bedroom and shower for the daughter. Unlike earlier Wright designs where kitchens were small and called workspaces, this area was quite large and included a walk-in pantry. To enter the house one walked past an unremarkable carport and squeezed through a small, confining tunnel. Then, literally shocking the senses, one emerged into a glorious, unobstructed vista of volcanoes, prairie, and ocean stretching to infinity. A simple glass door to the immediate left beckoned you to enter... and catch your breath.

The construction would feature coral aggregate concrete block, eight inches of concrete ground-level floors, large wooden glue-laminated beams, exposed wooden ceilings, built-in cherry wood cabinetry, large steel posts, and glass. A flat roof, treated with foam and elastomeric seal would cover the entire structure. It was a solid unit that could move as one piece over a compacted rock base in the event of an earthquake. This was seismic zone five, the maximum for the islands. Not too many years before, and not too many miles away, the island had experienced a quake 7.2 on the Richter scale. Witnesses said the ground moved like waves.

Floor plans for the Hawaii Island house first and second floor.

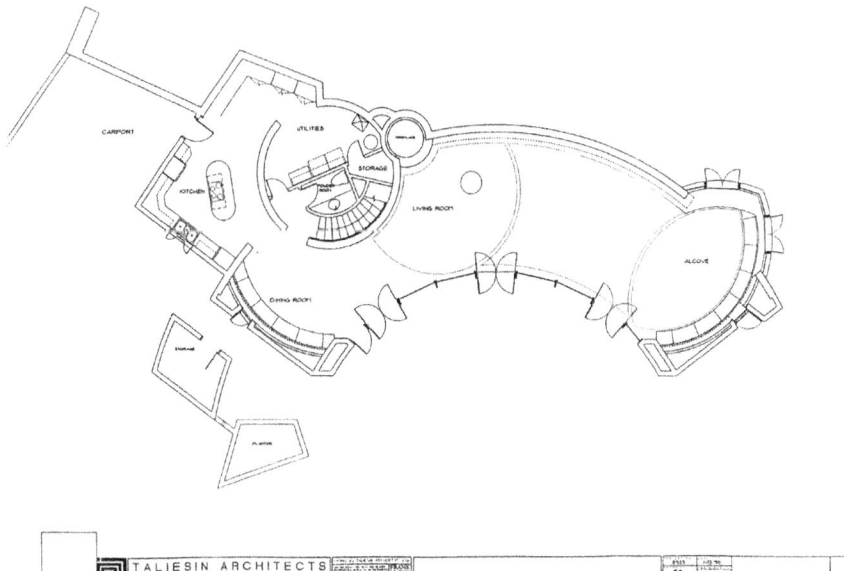

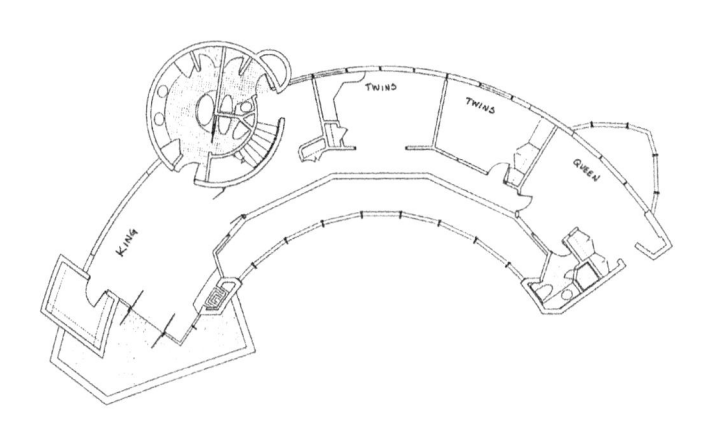

*"Synchronistic events provide
an immediate religious experience
as a direct encounter with the
compensatory patterning of events
in nature as a whole, both inwardly
and outwardly."*

Carl Jung

The Pregnancy Period

The house-planning now entered the period of "voodoo economics." Trying to figure costs was almost impossible. The plan was all curves, a nightmare to accurately calculate labor expenses. Figures for the first house existed, but this was an entirely different animal. I had read somewhere that a house designed by Wright would cost three times as much and take twice as long to build. I hoped to avoid this, and my plan was simple. Through the years I had become friends with Hans Torweihe, who could make anything with his hands. He had fallen for a local lady while visiting the islands, and married her. He had become a friend of my wife's best girlfriend, so it was inevitable that we would meet; when I learned that Hans had lived four years at Findhorn, the rapport was instant. I knew his values without hearing a word. He had skillfully remodeled our ad agency, figuring out how to "make do" and cut corners without ever sacrificing the needed quality. He smiled always, and if he were perplexed or challenged you would never be burdened. But more importantly, Hans seemed to be part of the rich weave of interconnectedness of this adventure. With his background and availability I felt he had been sent by my Invisible Partners.

Hans had separated from his wife and yearned for the quieter pace of an outer island when the idea of building this home took hold. He was part of my willingness to move forward. Not only was he enthusiastic, but I knew if there were any chance at all to tame the cost beast, it would be through Hans. He was to move to the island and live in a cottage I owned adjacent to the site. It was also near a completely equipped cabinetry shop. He'd get a salary, not an hourly wage. Not only would he wear the general contractor's hat, but he would build as much of the house by hand as possible. He could fabricate the furniture.

I needed a top-notch mason, someone good with laying brick and stone on the curve to build a house like this. I found a local contractor, Buck, in the next community. The cosmic unguent seemed to be easing my resistance. We pressed forward.

Hans ran detailed cost estimates, and figured the whole structure could be built for approximately $450,000. This was $200,000 less than the estimate for the Hargrove house; I was ready to go.

Out of the blue, Billy Gwynn, an old high school buddy, called me. He was in Honolulu with his wife, Quincie, to visit her mother. Over dinner, he told me that he had gone bankrupt as a commercial contractor. It seemed a little old lady with a lot of money defaulted. "I let my guard down," he said. "Tough lesson at this age."

As teenage buddies, we had both gone to parties in the Wright house owned by the Lewises. They were a banking family and patrons of the arts, and their house had always intrigued us both. I liked Billy a lot. Now completely bald, Billy was a strong, husky, impulsive guy who would jump up from the dinner table, recite poetry and dance "Zorba the Greek" for you. He studied to be a psychologist, but the performing arts pulled him away. He became a poet, doing readings primarily at universities. To pay the bills he had worked his way up in the construction trades: "slingin' mud," as he said.

I filled him in on the project, and showed him the plans. He didn't waste time. "Sandy," he asked, "who are you going to get to do that brickwork?"

"This guy Buck, but we still have some unanswered questions."

He paused, sensing an opening, and then looked directly at me and said, "Has he ever laid bricks on the curve?"

"I don't really know."

"Well I'm a master mason and I can tell you, this ain't no training job. No job to give to someone who has never laid a brick in the round, especially this house. I can do this job: and do it damned well," he said. "And one more thing. I'm ready to go. I could start tomorrow."

Another synchronicity. Billy was here, qualified, ready to work. The working drawings arrived that week. He saw them an hour after I did, and sent me a bid I couldn't refuse.

"Billy, it's all yours."

We began construction in earnest, in the spring of 1992. I was still living and working in Honolulu and running the third largest ad agency in the state. We were doing well. Susanne was happy in Honolulu, but saw that the house could be a showplace for new ideas. We valued the company of interesting people, and both of us had discussed how often we'd read books, been to lectures, or seen people on TV, and wondered what they were really like? Who inspired them? What had been their path? If there were a way we could attract these people, get to hang out together for a week or so, wouldn't that be something? Her idea was to create an institute and invite luminaries to spend a week in Hawaii, staying in a Frank Lloyd Wright house. We would pay them to mingle with a small group in Hawaii whom we would assemble from the mainland. They would pay us to meet people they probably would never have met. Everyone would be on vacation. The guest star would only have to speak during the morning, on anything he wanted to. The rest of the time would be free except for organized field trips. We wanted to stay in Honolulu, come over for the events, and rent the house out in-between. The dream pulled us forward.

The working drawings were completed, based on our local surveyor's input, and the building department approved the plans with only one small code change. We were ready to go.

*"Let no feeling of discouragement
prey upon you, and in the end
you are sure to succeed."*

Abraham Lincoln

Courtesy Carolyn Blake Photography

Construction Begins

The lengthy spreadsheet with the carefully itemized spending categories sat before me. Hans and I had carefully reviewed each item. The very first one, land-clearing, had a $5,000 figure beside it. A hole had to be dug for a cesspool, and some blue rock would be broken up and removed. On the bright side, the site was fairly level. It looked to me like this part would be smooth sailing.

To commemorate the start I flew over to meet with the clearing contractor. A beaten up hoe ram and equally sad bulldozer sat under a tree. I was given a good daily rate and told that our man was reliable. Several feet needed to be taken off. I thought we could be done in a week. After an informal chat about what he planned to do, we shook hands. He climbed on the bulldozer, fired it up, and the earth began to move.

Bulldozers give the appearance of immediate progress: lots of material is pushed about, and it makes one feel confident. The plan was to clear away the dirt, and see just how much rock had to be removed. Slowly large outcroppings were revealed. One large relatively smooth rock caught our attention. Little by little, more and more of the dirt was scraped away until, to our great astonishment, a completely round two-ton boulder sat in front of us. It must have been spewed from one of the lava vents eons ago.

A helper appeared and the hoe ram was fired up. It had a long hinged arm with a steel protrusion, acting like a huge metal woodpecker's beak. The incessant staccato noise was deafening, and I knew the neighbors would be very unhappy.

By the end of the first week, all of the easy dirt had been removed. Hans told me the amount of blue rock still unbroken was sizeable. Two more weeks passed, and the hoe ram broke down. Nothing happened on the site until it was fixed. A couple more weeks went by, and the ram was back at it, making progress ever so slowly. My bill had grown to $20,000.

Only one site for the septic tank would do. Any other location required pumping raw sewage uphill. I was told that it would be an eternal nightmare and needed to be avoided at all costs.

"How about dynamite?" I asked Hans.

"No, no. No way," he said. "The site could instantly become too unstable. It would compromise the foundations."

The hoe ram came back to work, and Hans began the delicate task of jackhammering the cesspool. He could hammer down a foot a day in a hole twelve feet in diameter. At the end of each day we were one foot deeper, and $1,000 poorer. Day after day I chewed my nails. Finally, twelve days later he hit soft dirt, the kind you need for drainage. We were done! I got down on my hands and knees to give thanks, and the hoe ram broke down again. The next-door neighbors said they were under siege. Karma was building, but eight weeks later the site was cleared. The $5,000 line item was now $42,000, and no construction had begun. My nerves were shot, and we'd barely begun.

My surveyor called. "Sandy, I've made a big mistake on my calculations. We've taken out too much dirt and rock. We're much deeper than we ought to be. I hate to say it, but we have to fill and compact." He paused. "You could sue me and the insurance company will probably pick up most of it," he said.

My mind raced ahead. How much more? But I was determined not to sue. I wasn't starting a job that way. It was time to move on. Another $8,000 later, the site was filled and compacted. We were ready to start. My $5,000 line item had increased to $50,000.

Billy gave me a firm bid for the foundation and all of the brickwork. Originally, the plans called for fieldstone: easily available in Pennsylvania but not in Hawaii, where lava rock abounded. John said no to that idea. Way too dark for an interior, so concrete block appeared to be the answer. We looked at several options. One was to use a split-face finish on both sides, instead of only one. The split surface was rough, as if the block had been broken; to a degree, it mimicked a stone surface. Or, we could have used a simple four-inch by four-inch by sixteen-inch plain smooth block. There was a concrete block factory only fifteen miles away. Yet, their block was made from blue rock, still too dark. Fortunately, Honolulu had a large supply of block still made from the coral dredged to create the famous reef runway, an alternative landing site for the space shuttle. It seemed to be the answer. The coral radiated a warm organic softness, nurturing, as opposed to the harder feel of stone or rock. After all, it once was alive. Perhaps the walls would echo those once radiant life forms. Since it was to be a major feature of the house (virtually all of the walls would be left bare), choosing the right kind of block was essential. John liked the smooth four-inch high block. The cost, including the shipping, turned out to be reasonable. It was a go.

The small crew included Mario Obra, a draftsman, who wanted the thrill of building the house. Mario knew everyone in the local trades and county planning department, a good person to have aboard. First, a large pole went up in the center of the front lawn, symbolic in one sense of a conductor's wand. All measurements were to be taken from this pole, ensuring that the curved lines of the outer walls would be accurate. Billy and the crew moved with assurance. The foundations went in smoothly, followed by a working concrete floor. Four inches deep, it spread out like the surface of a skating rink, and appeared deceptively large at first. Billy calmed me. "It's just right," he said. "Once the walls go up, you'll see."

Next, a rubberized membrane was rolled on, a black filling. Four more inches of concrete were to be added. The top slab would be poured in sections divided by metal expansion joints: all of this would prevent cracking in case of an earthquake. This was a seismic zone five and measurements above seven points on the Richter scale occurred. Later, engineers told me that the compacted fill we now had might actually be the best. In a big quake, the house would move as a unit, sliding back and forth on the fill. Reflecting, I thought about the surveyor's mistake. Maybe it wasn't a mistake, but another synchronistic event. He unknowingly had forced us into the best house foundation.

By this time, John was not as comfortable with my innocence as I was. He was troubled by not having a general contractor. He felt a construction manager would save us money and perhaps avoid real glitches.

"Sandy," John said, "I'd like you to meet Robert West. He managed the construction process for the Maui clubhouse, and did an impressive job. He might be of some real help." Translation: hire Robert. He was no stranger to these designs. Not only had he just finished the Maui clubhouse, he built the house Wright designed for Vincent Sculley, the well-known architectural critic. We met, and I liked Robert. Soon, he was part of our team.

As time passed, I learned that the curving nature of the house probably would have kept any good contractor from making a firm bid. Most would have taken it on a "cost plus" basis. It would have been impossible to determine accurately how long the job might take. A contractor forced to bid might quote too high for protection against the unknown, and too low a bid might have resulted in shoddy work.

The building site sat unprotected from the unrelenting wind. It could play havoc with your concentration, and your moods. Billy figured his end of the job would take six months. Yet his estimate of 200 blocks laid a day dropped to seventy-five. "Hell Sandy," he said, "that wind's a bitch! It blew so hard today, it pushed a hammer clear across the cement floor. I've never seen anything like it."

The curves in the walls required some ninety percent of the sixteen-inch blocks to be hand cut on the site: a requirement that had evaded all of our calculations. Hans, like a squad leader in a fire fight, immediately jumped in as the block cutter. He developed the muscles in his right arm to prove it.

The long block, Billy explained, was the most difficult to lay. It had to be absolutely level. A small variance at the beginning would become unacceptably large at the other end. A few walls were torn down for this reason. Slowly, day by day, the circular brickwork rose, taking on the shape of a medieval castle ruin. Neighbors and curiosity-seekers stopped by to gawk, and everyone seemed to sense the special form being birthed into existence, one they had never seen.

Steel columns stood tall in the front of the house, ready to cradle the large glue-laminated beams jutting out like radial spokes from notches in the back wall. These beams would not only support the roof, but would also allow the second floor to hang from the ceiling. Invisible rods bolted through the ceiling beams into the floor supports would achieve the illusion that the second floor floated in space.

We ordered our materials from the West Coast through a Seattle broker, and everything was to be inspected before being containerized. Robert provided shop drawings to the mill fabricating the glue-laminated beams, and these were built up strip by strip. Then they were cut with a camber: that is, they would appear to be bowed upon arrival. As the weight of the second floor and roof were added, the beams were supposed to straighten out perfectly. It turned out that having Robert and a good broker was a godsend. The broker found that sixty percent of the beams were six inches too short. Robert rejected them and ordered them to be replaced. The mill refused. The broker took them to court. The judge ordered the mill to redo the job.

A monster crane arrived, and slowly the beams were gently notched into the back wall on the rear end, and into the steel column cradles on the front end. The house now looked like a skeleton.

Into our second year, the framing, flooring and window construction seemed to settle into some never-ending routine, as if time had been suspended everywhere except on the checkbook. The job had become a work of art. A standard of excellence emerged, created and treasured by the workers themselves. It was unspoken, but expected from everyone. It was a very difficult house to build. Even though there was a full set of working drawings, creative decisions had to be made daily.

Billy pulled me aside one day.

"Sandy, Hans spends a lot of time in his truck, driving around to pick up things. Other people could pick that stuff up. Hell, you could even have it delivered. You might want to speak to him about it. I've seen lots of money disappear that way."

I confronted Hans after work. He looked down embarrassed, and said, "Billy's right, I often do go out to get materials. Truth is I'm stumped. I need time in the truck to figure out what to do next."

I was the one who felt embarrassed. If there was one thing that Hans was not, it was lazy. We experienced our encounter as purely innocent. We both knew everyone's intentions were good. It was a work that demanded the best from all of us, and I never questioned him again.

I knew better. Hans had actually fabricated certain connections not even in the plans, but absolutely essential. Even Billy often added more rebar, saying, "I don't care what the plans say, we gotta have it."

I felt blessed. These were good caring people.

Billy's work was ending. He'd been on the job twice as long as he had estimated. We walked the spaces. The basket weave appearance of the cylinder walls was enchanting. The expansive long back walls were smooth and even. The horizontal lines were exact and true. There was not a flaw to be found. It was simply masterful work. As we slowly walked off the site at dusk that evening, I swore we could hear the bricks saying, "Billy, we salute you."

Several years later, the house was given the "concrete achievement" award, a biannual recognition of the best work done in the islands. I kicked in a bonus, even though my money was almost gone. Work of this caliber deserved it.

I was almost broke by that point, but somehow not worried. Destiny seemed to be at work, as if the house had its own intention. Frank Lloyd Wright had designed a house for Judge Martin Pence years ago. It was to have been built in Hilo, just sixty-five miles or so away from this site. When the final estimates had arrived, double what Pence had in mind, he scrapped the project.

I was suddenly drawn away from the house. My father died, though we had long since said our good-byes. He had been in a nursing home for a little over a year, hanging on, but not really present. A series of strokes had taken their toll. The estate settled quickly, and I received another $400,000. Maybe that would see me through.

"By banishing doubt and trusting your intuitive feelings, you clear a space for the power of intention to flow through."

Wayne Dyer

CLOSING IN ON THE HOUSE

By now the basic shape was evident. It was going to be magnificent, much more so than the drawings. I felt that once the roof went on, and the glass windows were installed, it was almost complete. Seeing a roof on and windows in place gave me a false feeling that the house was done. That was far from the truth.

Our original plans and cost estimates called for a pitch and gravel roof; a flat roof with a small slope. John was now concerned that we might need a better roof, one that would allow for the coefficient of expansion between dissimilar materials. In poorly built houses or buildings you can often hear a groaning and creaking sound as the temperature increases. We all agreed: no groans. The solution was to use a foam spray. The foam, applied with a special gun, was built up in the front of the house and slowly tapered to allow for drainage. Drying rapidly, it was then covered with an elastomeric seal of liquid rubber, combined with a painted sand-like finish.

This was once a popular roof idea in Hawaii, many poorly executed jobs hit the market and architects shied away from it. Consequently there were virtually no foam roof contractors in the state. The crew was going to be flown in from Arizona. The job would only take a day, but weather conditions would have to be perfect: no wind. Furthermore, the decorative molding, made from fiberboard but looking like anodized copper, needed to be affixed as one unit when the foam was sprayed on. John had a Phoenix roofing company in mind.

The crew arrived. As a precaution, a protective temporary wind barrier was erected; it looked, at a distance, like a third story. One irate neighbor ran over protesting vigorously that there was a two-story height limitation.

My greatest concern was safety. Gusting winds could easily have sent someone sailing, especially if they were holding any large flat surfaces. No sooner had I had this thought than a crew member gingerly picked up a four by eight sheet of plywood and was caught by the wind; and he was blown off the back side of the roof. Luckily he fell only a short distance onto the berm. His dislocated shoulder sobered the crew, but even with the barrier up, the winds were too strong. Several days passed, and then like the calm in the eye of a storm, it was time. The spray gun compressor cranked up, and the soft foam gently settled. The fascia and final application fell seamlessly into place. The roof was finally on. Looking at the fascia, I felt the archetypal presence of a council of elders. Wright had left his mark.

After several setbacks, our glass supplier obtained the tint we required. One of Wright's signature treatments was a mitered glass corner. Two pieces of glass from different angles were joined together with a clear epoxy. To the eye it appeared to be one piece of glass. The effect was most prominent in the large alcove area at the far end of the house. There, like the bow of a boat, the mitered glass rose two stories. The view from the alcove area was to the stream flowing downhill toward the house. On a day when the water was raging, the site was spectacular. Large boulders could bound down, sending tremors through the ground and house, reminding you the gods were present.

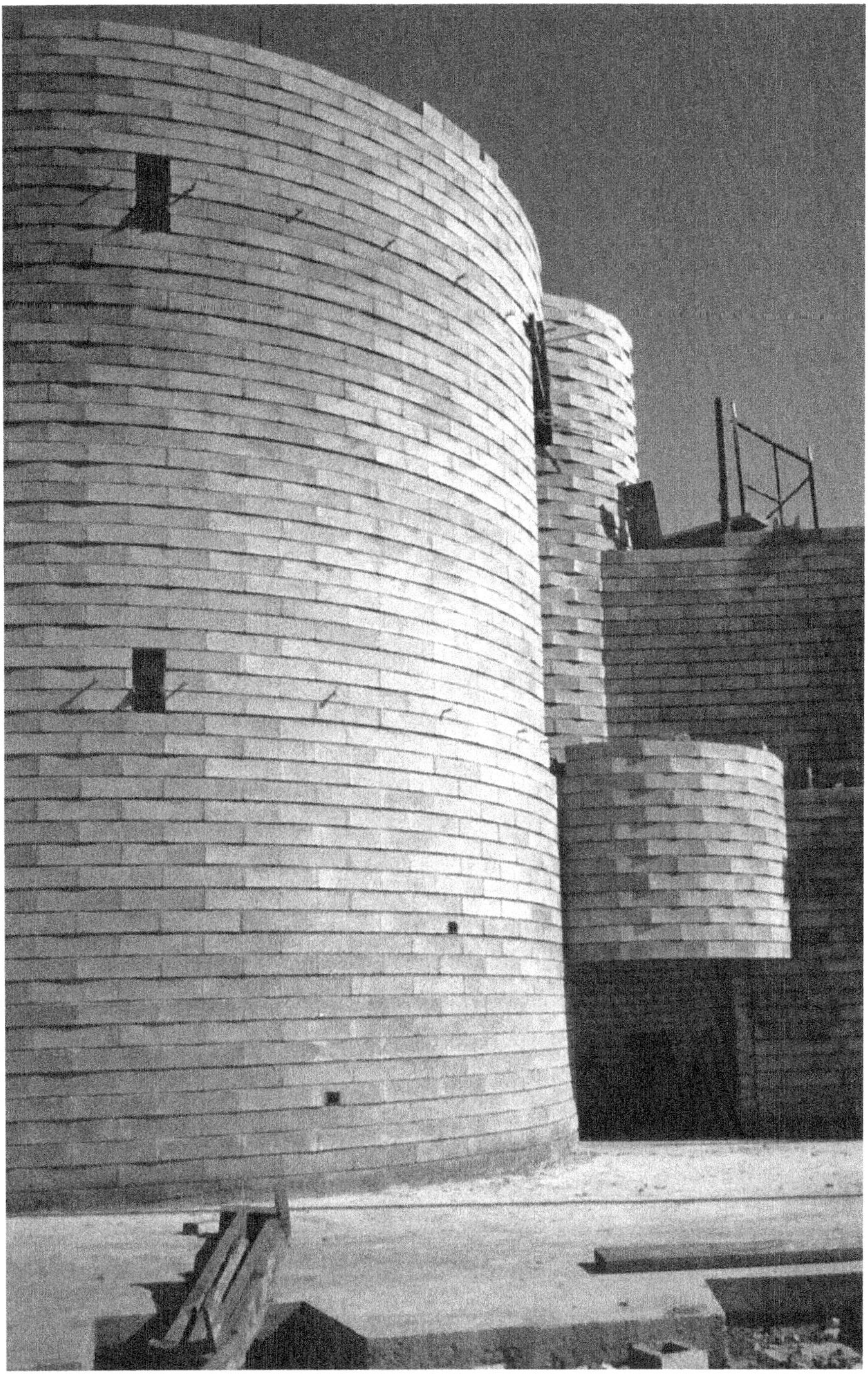

*"Success comes from taking the
initiative and following up... persisting...
eloquently expressing the depth of your love.
What simple action could you take today
to produce a new momentum toward success
in your life?"*

Tony Robbins

The Universe Provides

I still had about $250,000 left, and somehow from my past experiences I felt that things would work out. I just was not prepared for the next development.

My phone rang as I walked into my Honolulu office.

"Hi Sandy, Don here. You got a few minutes? I need to see you," he said.

"Sure, Don, come on down."

A few moments later Don strode in briskly and sat down, determined but nervous.

"I've been here over twenty years," he said. "You've been running the agency for all of that time. It's my turn. I need my chance. I want to buy you out. If you're not willing to do this, perhaps Lynne and I should leave, and try our mettle elsewhere."

Don, for all of those years, had loyally remained in the shadow. Around town, he had a reputation as a marketing expert, as well as a top athlete. For several years he would run 17 miles in the morning to the office before the workday began. The New Age spiritual movement had swept him into a close relationship with Marshall Thurber, a founder of the "Business and You" seminars. Don's dedication and determination had made him a candidate to succeed Marshall, but his guardedness allowed the job to pass on to someone else.

"That's it?" I said quietly. "That's it," he answered. He quickly rose, turned and walked out. I was stunned, not quite sure for a moment what happened. I felt vulnerable, hollow, and maybe even resentful.

Don's wife, Lynne, was in charge of client services. The clients all loved her, and so did the staff. We had an employee stock ownership plan, and the agency had accumulated a sizeable amount of cash. It was all part of an exit strategy for the senior partners and an orderly transition to the next generation. Small regional ad agencies are extremely difficult to sell to outsiders. Ultimately, the employees are the best bet, but somehow, I just was not ready. It seemed too abrupt. Yet I had been slowly disappearing, purposely making others more prominent and more important. Don did have a valid point: as much as we had been preparing for this transition we had never firmed a date. I was comfortable. Perhaps too comfortable.

Was he really ready, or was this just my way of procrastinating? I had a river of emotions. I was angry, but at what? That he had initiated this change rather than me? That as the leader I should have been the one to decide? Maybe his actions did show leadership. It was decisive. He deserved a chance to succeed or fail on his own terms. Maybe it was time to go. He had been loyal, and I could have been the one dragging my feet.

Events certainly were conspiring to help me. I needed money to finish the house. There it was. I had slowly been preparing for a change, and now it had come. If this were the work of my Invisible Partners, the style might have been abrupt, but I couldn't deny the results. The wounds allowed waves of anger, despair, resentment, judgment and insecurity to crash through. Frantically, I clung to an interior lifeboat until the storm subsided. Finally there was inner calm. It was time for me to move on.

We called Scott Smith, a financial consultant with Worldwide Partners, a group of advertising agencies from around the world of which we were a member. Scott was a big guy, an ex-arena football coach and CPA wunderkind, and his complete honesty and genuineness was instantly recognized by everyone. He spoke with an authority that conveyed wisdom beyond his years. We agreed to accept, without question, his verdict.

He flew out, evaluated the agency, and set up the buyout. In a few short weeks, the deal was done. I was given more than the stock price to compensate for my agreeing to leave early and thereby forfeiting future retirement contributions. Don was ecstatic. His bold move gave him complete control of the state's 3rd largest agency, one rich in cash and at the height of its reputation.

It was the end of 1994. There was no question now of lacking enough money to finish the house. As before, the resources didn't arrive at the eleventh hour, but before. I could feel the presence of other forces. It was as if the house was consciously attracting what it needed to complete itself.

Part of my arrangement was to maintain an office in Honolulu, and Susanne and I stayed for a while but the Big Island called. We rented our Honolulu house and moved to our cottage a few hundred yards away from the construction. On the site now every day, I helped where needed. My hands were in the dirt, and it felt good. I was following some deeper current and was on course.

For Susanne, at 36, the move was daunting, because she was a true city girl. The buzz of the city was a life-supporting energy. It fed her needs as an aspiring career woman. She enjoyed the success of being the salesperson of the year for a national travel publication, of launching an environmental public relations firm and becoming a recognized international public speaker. Honolulu was her city and her home, but a small country town on the Big Island was pulling her away from the city energy that had sustained her. To compensate, she threw herself vigorously into starting the "New Millennium Institute," her name for the organization that would run the small luminary programs, once the Frank Lloyd Wright home was completed.

She lined up a group of well-known experts that included Raymond Moody, the psychiatrist who had become well known for his work on near-death experiences; Terence McKenna, a protégé of Timothy Leary's; Matthew Fox, the controversial priest who had been excommunicated; Edgar Mitchell, the sixth man to walk on the moon; Hank Wesselman, an anthropologist and authority on Hawaiian shamanism; and finally John and Kay Rattenbury, to talk about living and working with Frank Lloyd Wright.

In the spring of '95, John arrived to review the work. He was extremely pleased with the level of craftsmanship, but concerned about the overall momentum. Robert West had left, feeling he could no longer save us any money.

Susanne told John about the plans for the use of the house, and that in March her programs were to start. John, tongue in cheek, smiled and said, "What year?" The silence was deafening.

Susanne blurted out, "Next year!" The fear of her programs failing, and the isolation of this rural setting haunted her.

"Not the way it's progressing now," John said softly. "You're years away, especially if Hans has to fabricate the interior. The large doors for the front of the house haven't been made yet either."

Susanne stared at me. It felt not like a gentle request, but a fierce silent command.

From the very beginning, Hans and I had planned on his fabricating all of the built-in furnishings, using the carpentry shop a few hundred yards away. Synchronicity came to the rescue. John and I put our heads together. Hawaii was stagnant. Real estate prices on the Big Island were in the doldrums, high-end properties were languishing, and skilled laborers and craftsman were looking for work.

John had bid on the cabinetry in Arizona. With these numbers, we visited Roy Lambrecht in Kailua-Kona, the bustling tourist community thirty miles away. Roy's cabinetry shop was known for superb work. Entering the workspace I could almost hear the large sophisticated machines greeting us and sending us telepathic mantras, "We're available. We're good. We can save you time." John liked Roy, a pleasant easy-going guy. As Roy looked at the plans, he noted the ten-foot doors, and transom windows over each pair of doors, and the front door. Essentially this was the entire front of the house. Looking up from the plans, Roy said, "I can save you a lot of time and cost by fabricating the entire front of the house in my shop. Furthermore, I can build the alcoves for the dining room and far end of the living room, living room wall cabinets, beds, built-in desks and some furniture."

The next day Roy was back with numbers that were competitive with the Arizona shop's figures. John asked Roy if there was anything that could reduce the costs further.

"Cut out the requirement to make shop drawings and I can knock off another $14,000," Roy answered.

"Done," John said.

By the time we left Roy's shop for the second time, everything he had offered to do, even the perplexing handrail needed for the stairwell to the second floor, was now in his hands.

"Sandy, when did you say you wanted the house done?" John said.

"John," I laughed, "the really good news is we're going to tell Susanne the mountains have been moved."

Hans' eyes lit up with the news. He was visibly relieved.

Roy called John to discuss making the stiles, the wood frames holding the glass on the front door, wider to accommodate the hardware. "No, can't do that, Roy," John said. "It will alter the look and character of the house. This is exactly why the Taliesin Associated Architects retain all architectural rights to the building of Frank Lloyd Wright's plans." A few days later Roy dug a little deeper and found compatible hardware.

After seeing the house, Urse, Roy's shop foreman, decided to fabricate the pieces himself. I knew we'd made the right decision. "Urse is Swiss, very precise, and can swear at you in German," I told Hans. Hans laughed and gave me the thumbs up.

It was late in the morning several weeks later, and the rumbling of approaching trucks filled the air. Down the gravel driveway in a cloud of dust came the unassembled entire front of the house, three sets of double doors ten feet high, the transom windows and the front door. In two weeks, Hans would have the house completely closed in.

*"Live out of your imagination,
not your history."*

Stephen Covey

Courtesy Carolyn Blake Photography

Excellence Is Contagious

It was a pivotal moment: the pour of the final slab was the critical one. Billy was long gone, and Hans found a cement contractor friend who admitted he had never applied a "dust on" finish. In this technique, a dyed powder is sprinkled on and then worked into the wet cement with a trowel down to a level of two or so inches. When applied correctly, it gives the brightest finish.

Much rode on this task. It was "the finish." Robert had told me how at the Sculley house the dye had been mixed in the truck. This is referred to as an integral mix. The mixture, when poured, had come off "too hot," and the entire floor had to be jackhammered up and re-poured. I couldn't think about this, because too much had gone right. I had come to believe that even the consciousness of the house simply wouldn't let that happen.

We covered the entire space with an elastomeric rubber coating; it was a sea of black. Expansion strips were affixed via brackets to the floor, forming metal membrane-like sections. The concrete was poured slowly into each section, with the red-colored dye being sprinkled on by hand. The trowel in the hands of our contractor moved confidently and rhythmically. In no time it was completed. Once it was dry, a coat of wax was buffed on. Our red floor, now eight inches thick, glistened, radiated, and beckoned. It was simply beautiful. My eyes followed the dust of the contractor's truck as he disappeared down the road. Another angel had come and gone.

Shortly after, the fabricated alcoves arrived. One went into the dining area, the other into the far end of the living room. Each was a massive unit, over twenty feet long, made from solid cherry wood. Just rubbing it made me tingle. Urse gracefully slid these wooden beings into their new slots. The fit was so precise a razor couldn't pass between the brick and the wood.

We had looked at a variety of woods, including Koa, which is native to Hawaii. As much as we would have loved using this wood, the Koa would have darkened too much. The cabinetry for all of the rooms followed the cherry wood suit. Cherry, I was to learn, darkens in time, and then a few years later begins to lighten. Each element of Urse's repertoire was exquisitely done.

Upstairs, Hans showed me spots where the floor squeaked.

"What will it take to correct that?" I asked.

"Another layer of three-quarter-inch plywood."

"Over the spots, or the whole second floor?"

"The whole floor," he quietly said.

"How much?"

"Another $5,000."

I nodded.

This was the ritual.

It was also indicative of the extra costs that could not have been fathomed in the beginning. We didn't know that the floors would squeak. They did. We didn't know if there would be heat gain on the second floor. There wasn't. Exhaust fans were installed as a precaution, anyway.

The bathrooms carried the same tile and color, small squares of sea foam green, as if they were interchangeable. John pointed out that while subtle, these elements supported a sense of unity in the overall design. You could only be in one bathroom at a time, but the memory created an integration, a sense that there was a design unit.

Large rolls of beige wool carpeting would be laid to cover virtually all of the upstairs floors, excluding the bathrooms. Downstairs they would be cut and sewn, on-site, to form area rugs. The wide red cement border would form the complementary accent.

The last crucial element was the lighting. Light boxes were built into the alcoves and the long living room shelf. Rope lights were installed behind opaque Plexiglass box covers, and under the living room shelf, so as to wash the wall. On dimmer switches, the rope lights could alter the mood of the entire space. The balance of the lighting was achieved with track spotlights and sconces.

Wright had loved the warmth of the autumn palette. The red floor, cherry woodwork, and beige carpeting revealed the wisdom of this combination, especially as the day turned to evening, and the subtle accent lights added a golden glow.

While the house seemed to be going up extremely smoothly, other forces were mounting to test us.

"Life is a series of natural and spontaneous changes. Don't resist them — that only creates sorrow. Let reality be reality. Let things flow naturally forward in whatever way they like."

Lao Tzu

Courtesy Carolyn Blake Photography

THE NEIGHBORHOOD REBELS,
WHILE THE HOUSE GOES TO THE BEAUTY PARLOR

Susanne had begun to advertise for the first seminar with Raymond Moody. Since the house had several bedrooms, part of the plan was to host a few of the seminar attendees, with others staying in various nearby guest accommodations. An ad was placed. A next-door neighbor complained saying that this activity was a zoning violation, and needed a special use permit.

The special use permit required neighborhood approval. Polarization arose. People were fearful the house would become a continuing tourist attraction, inviting non-stop traffic. Some were opposed based on the idea that the programs looked to be too controversial. There were organized neighborhood meetings and Susanne was devastated. She felt blind-sided. Even though we were among the very first to own land in this five-acre subdivision, we were portrayed as city slickers who thought they could just waltz in and do anything they wanted. The neighborhood polarized, escalating into public hearings where I really got to experience what fear could produce. In the end, the Planning Commission granted the permit, allowing the house to be used for a certain number of educational seminars annually.

Unfortunately, the resisting residents didn't accept this ruling. They filed a suit charging that seminars and overnight guest accommodations violated the neighborhood covenants. This second round was even more maddening, as the ante was raised. Now it was courts, attorneys, plenty of money, and more anguish.

Susanne had never wanted to leave Honolulu; she did so only to follow my dream, and me. Now the one common focus for this home's use was under siege.

The house was moving into the finishing stages. The kitchen cabinetry arrived, and I remember Roy calling and saying, "Sandy, you'll need to hire an installer."

This was one of those dark holes in home construction that was invisible to me.

"Well yes, of course, I thought, oh I see. You mean that requires someone else other than you? Oh, OK. You have an installer? His name is Jerry? OK, good, I'll give him a ring."

By now my budget and worksheets looked bad, though I had wanted to build this house for the sheer joy and desire of experiencing what it might bring. I liked to think my Invisible Partners simply would not let it fail. What was evident was that resources had arrived more like a gusher than a trickle.

Jerry Stutz, when not riding bulls in major competitions, installed. "Installation" became my new favorite word. Jerry was jovial, fun, humorous, spontaneous and attached to a saw, drill, and measuring tape. He and his crew were like dervishes; power tools buzzed and banged, doors were hung, and trim was fabricated. Kitchen and bathroom cabinetry went in; Hans was all over the place, taking care of small hardware, managing painters, plumbers, and electricians.

I said to Jerry as he finished up, "I didn't even know how to spell the word install before you showed up, but now, $30,000 later, I really understand it."

Jerry grinned on his way out, "Anytime you need help, call me."

By this time, Susanne was not the enthusiastic, fun-loving city girl I remembered. Madam Pele, goddess of the volcanoes, was having her way. People say that the island of Hawaii draws you here to face your issues. It is raw creative energy expressing itself in a perpetual state of eruption.

We were both facing it. Even though the house was now exceeding the budget by a factor of three, Susanne was adamant about adding some amenities. A hot tub, made to look like a natural pool would be a fitting addition she thought. John agreed.

I found an old friend, John Groark, whose company specialized in building natural pools and waterscapes. The promenade, jutting out above the stream beyond the far alcove, would be the perfect setting; soaking under the Milky Way would be pure heaven. The island sky was crystal clear most nights. In the distance you could see the observatories atop Mauna Kea, a long extinct volcano. Reputedly, it housed more telescope glass than anywhere else in the world.

Since it was crunch time, I joined the crew in digging the hole. It actually turned out to be a mini swimming pool, complete with a heater and jets.

I asked John to make it look as good when it was empty, as when it was full.

The idea here was that, when dry, it should look like the empty seasonal streambed in the background. The crew was masterful in fabricating rocks to mimic what was naturally there. Acid Man, the name I had secretly given him, stepped in at the end to gouge holes and make striated crack marks in the wet cement. Dark brown and rust streaks formed, as the acid mixture was applied and seeped into the cement. The line between man and nature's work blurred. Four weeks later, we were basking in bubbling hot water, as if it were the earth's own hot spring.

The front yard had been planted with a winter-type grass, but we gave each other the "not good enough" look. I went in search of something with more pizzazz. Japanese "bump" grass turned out to be the ticket. Slow growing, it would actually grow on top of itself if not cut. Two weeks later the bump grass sod was rolled into place — instant greenery! The focal point, a stone Buddha from Bali, gazed across the new lawn to the living room and the spherical boulder, sitting on the cement walkway where it was first discovered.

Soon, the furniture was delivered, some of it from Arizona and some from Italy. Since this was to be a focus home showing Frank Lloyd Wright's presence in Hawaii, we decided to enhance the experience by using as many of Wright's furniture designs as possible. The dining room alcove used the barrel chairs from Chicago's Robie house. They were made under license from Cassina, in Italy. In the living room, Taliesin wing chairs accented with red cushions surrounded a large, round coffee table. Two love seats and a large Prairie style desk filled out the room. Moveable hassocks, a favorite of Wright's, lined the wall. At the entrance stood two gorgeous Taliesin floor lamps. I could almost feel the presence of the great architect. He would have been proud.

The fireplace was huge. I had to bend myself into its cavernous space. Fires can transfix, seduce, capture and transport us to places we forget about in our daily lives. Large fireplaces are like large movie screens, enveloping us completely into the story. Several evenings were spent in front of the hypnotic blaze, but at times we heard howling wind blocking the chimney vent. In the end we converted to gas logs. It was still wonderful.

A private entrance took you around a bend to one of Wright's metal gates. It led you down a short curving road with a tree-lined berm on the right, and large ironwood trees to the left. The eye would first see only a berm and the clerestory windows of the second floor. For the most part the house was hidden. The driveway wound down to the right, and then to the left to the carport. Off to the right were trees blocking the view. The portal was dead ahead. You passed through double glass doors, and a planter on the right. Then suddenly, the view exploded into a grand vista of three volcanoes and the ocean. You turned to the left and the full panorama of two stories of glass and the broad curving overhang greeted your eye.

Courtesy Carolyn Blake Photography

"Cease trying to work everything out with your minds. It will get you nowhere... Live by intuition and inspiration and let your whole life be a revelation."

Eileen Caddy

A Masterpiece

No words could convey the deep love and appreciation I felt for Hans. He had worked tirelessly for almost four years, solving challenges and problems we never knew existed. He never complained; nor for that matter even showed any irritation.

The house had been almost completed before the critical March deadline. John gave the effort and workmanship an A+. It was indeed a work of art, no less than a masterpiece. It was solid, tight, and for the most part, soundproof. It had survived three earthquakes in the 5.0 range on the Richter scale without a hitch. The trade winds sailed over the berm and roof, leaving the front area calm and peaceful. There was no heat gain on the second floor. The inside temperature was perfect on both floors, day and night. No air conditioning or heating was ever required.

Each gaze revealed some new magical intersection of geometry.

At $1.2 million, it had cost two and half times as much as I thought it would. Most of my cost saving efforts had been ambushed at some part of the journey. The pundits who had said Wright homes would take twice as long and cost three times as much as I planned were right. Yet, the money had arrived, steadily and assuredly. I had wanted the pure experience of building it. I had gotten it. In spite of my naiveté, forces had conjoined not only to complete it, but to complete it perfectly. I could not have anticipated the timing, the skillful people who showed up, the money, and finally the grace with which it took place. To my Invisible Partners, thank you...

Standing on the second floor, looking past the curvature of the roof to the distance, I felt I could be on the bridge of the Starship Enterprise.

The house was ready. For me it was the pure satisfaction of creating a stunning piece of artwork. It was not just a house, it was an expression of one of the greatest artists of our time. Now on this remarkable landscape stands an enduring example of what magnificent architecture could do for the human spirit. It was a fulfillment that enriched my life journey. For Susanne it was a beginning, a chance to harvest the rich potential human experience created by the intersection of Hawaii, Frank Lloyd Wright, and the luminaries this combination could attract.

Courtesy Carolyn Blake Photography

Courtesy Carolyn Blake Photography

"The spread of civilization may be likened to a fire; First, a feeble spark, next a flickering flame, then a mighty blaze, ever increasing in speed and power."

Nikola Tesla

John and Kay Rattenbury (3rd and 4th from left) and seminar attendees

Let The Retreats Begin —
Visits From The Other Side, The Inner Astronaut And The Outer Astronaut

Dr. Raymond Moody was light-hearted, fascinating and fun, and Susanne had organized a welcome dinner, followed by a presentation in town, open to the community. The small group of twenty began their private seminar the following morning. Fitting snugly into the alcove, people seemed to hang on to Raymond's every word. He was completely present with whomever he spoke with.

Having told us how much he loved rocking chairs, we located one for him. After about an hour of talking and rocking one lady said, "Raymond, I can't bob and write. I'm dizzy." We all were. We'd bonded, and Raymond gave up the rocking chair.

A psychiatrist by training, Raymond's fame came from his books on near death experiences. He had interviewed thousands of people. A consciousness explorer, like so many true scientists, he needed a way to fend off the skeptic label of being a kook. His answer was to teach logic at the University of Virginia.

He said believers and unbelievers were exactly the same. Both were passionately committed to a point of view that couldn't be proved.

"I find," he continued, "It's easier to say I'm a non-believer, open to ideas without having to make a commitment.

We discussed the idea that perhaps history was rewritten by the ruling powers to perpetuate its control over the population. As western materialism developed, prevailing spiritual practices seemed to give way to religious dogma. In ancient Greece, Raymond pointed out, it was common practice for individuals and families to seek dialogue with the deceased in underground temples known as "psychomanteums." There were literally hundreds of these in Greece. Counseling was the goal, much as one seeks counseling from trusted friends, or a therapist.

People would enter the temple for weeks or more. Very large metal containers in the shape of shallow bowls several feet across held oil. Under low candlelight, individuals and families would sit gazing into this speculum of oil. In time, apparitions of relatives or close family friends who had passed away would appear. And regular dialogue would take place between the living and the spirit of the deceased. It was the reality of the time.

Raymond pointed out that while this practice has long since vanished from the modern world, evidence of its existence is with us daily. People on their deathbeds, in their last days or moments, often pass back and forth between realities. We frequently refer to it as being delirious. He felt that society would at some point re-engage with these past but dormant capabilities.

As a hands on group project, we created our own psychomanteum below the stairwell, in a little storeroom, completely dark. We had no oil, but replicated the same effect by placing mirrors in strategic locations. A comfortable low canvas beach chair allowed you to easily relax. Candles were lit and each person had a chance to spend a half an hour or so, and report to the group. My turn came and I entered, relaxed and waited. Perhaps too much was going on for me. The time flew, and nothing seemed to happen. Yet, amazingly, about half of the group reported experiences. Everybody loved Raymond and his wife Cheryl, and they in return found the low-key gathering easy and comfortable, and the setting wonderful. The program model seemed to be good.

Susanne and I decided to be caretakers, living in the house as lightly as possible, almost as if we were working guests. Yet we didn't really settle in. The house was completely furnished for whomever was there, without our personal belongings. I wanted to experience the energy patterns created by the mystical genius of Frank Lloyd Wright. For Susanne, the house was more of a symbol; it placed her living in a country environment she could tolerate, but not embrace. For her, the house became a business. She saw it in terms of costs. To cut down on them, she cleaned incessantly. I wanted to help out by making sure we had cleaning people, but she had the sense that it was a business that was not making it. Perhaps I was oblivious while she suffered. Her unhappiness was masked; for some days she was cheerful and spontaneous. On other days, the mood barometer dropped suddenly. I ignored it, hoping it would go away, or better yet, that a new Susanne was emerging.

Terence McKenna, our next luminary, was not only a crowd-pleaser, but also a gift. Having attended his lectures, both Susanne and I were enamored fans. While known more as a protégé of Timothy Leary, and for his ethno-botanical journeys into the psychedelic realms, Terence's photographic mind, thirst for knowledge, immense vocabulary, and sense of humor made him one of the most remarkable human beings I'd ever met. The beauty of his language, the elegance of his thought processes and his limitless wellspring of knowledge made anything he said immensely seductive. One could not help leaving preconceived ideas or judgments at the door. As a guest said, "I don't care what he says. His language is pure poetry. I just want to hear him speak."

One of my favorite experiences with him at the house involved a group of Japanese visitors whose afternoon meeting with him was to learn about the effects of the sacred healing plant, ayahuasca. Accompanying the group was a somewhat nouveau riche boyfriend of a younger woman. He was dismissive and condescending toward Terence. At one point as if to fully discredit Terence, he said, "Why do you have to use the crutch of psychedelics? I meditate. That takes me to wonderful spaces. It isn't necessary to do more."

Terence reflected on the comment, and then said to him,

"I, too, meditate and also achieve those wonderful states you refer to, but it is totally in feeling. I see nothing. I am not here to urge anyone to take or do anything. However, Plato said that truth, beauty and goodness were one in the same. I have a difficult time discerning what is ultimately true or good, but I can recognize beauty. When I take psychedelics in a respectful and sacred manner, I am transported to interior landscapes of unimaginable and immense beauty. That is why I take them."

Terence had graciously and elegantly dealt with this man, merely explaining what was authentic for him. He did not belittle him, nor his experiences.

Terence was deeply appreciative of the house space. A young man who had come to the first seminar said to Terence, "I thought we were going to have some drug experiences here."

Terence answered, "I think it would be hardly fair to put these kind people (referring to Susanne and myself) out of business before they have actually gotten started."

An inner astronaut, journeying and recording the nature of his travels, Terence spoke from pure experience about the nature of realms he had visited. One morning his lecture turned to dimethyltryptamine, DMT, one of the most powerful of the hallucinogens.

"It transported me," he said, "and in a repeatable pattern, to a place where the Elfins, small people, reside. I was fascinated by the archetypal geometric forms emerging from their mouths as they spoke to one another."

While it fascinated Terence, the Elfin land held no personal interest for me. My own experience with psychedelics in the past had been that boundary disorientation of any kind only reaffirmed my profound appreciation for the miracle of this reality. And that realization alone made my few trips there worth it.

We spent a number of days discussing his Timewave Zero theory, about which he jokingly stated, "I should either be awarded the Nobel Prize or committed to an asylum."

Terence was the architect of Novelty Theory, which tries to show the ebb and flow of novelty in the universe as a quality of time. He postulated that there was slightly more novelty or newness in the universe than the opposite force of static habituation. When this novelty is graphed over time, a fractal wave form known as the time wave results. Terence referred to the Mayan calendar date of 2012 as the culmination or the eschaton. As one approaches the eschaton, the fractal patterns repeat faster and faster, until the culmination of what took eons of time in the beginning repeats itself in a nanosecond at the end.

We enjoyed speculating about what the end might look like: everything from the other side of the Big Bang to a massive change in consciousness.

Terence loved the house and conducted many seminars there in a very short time. Not long after, he was diagnosed with a rare brain cancer and died within a year. Just before his passing he came for the New Year's Eve 2000 party. In a moment of reverence and utter silence just before midnight, Terence stepped out on the master bedroom balcony to share his final thoughts.

"I have come to this house many times in its brief existence. It is here that I have experienced some of my most profound and finest thinking. Thank you."

Terence had found the powerful presence Frank Lloyd Wright had created.

• • •

We looked up at the full moon as Edgar pointed to it and described his landing.

My bare feet sank into the cool, damp grass and my eyes were riveted on the almost full moon. I shivered with goose bumps. My mouth dropped open and my eyes dilated. I quietly pinched myself, not in disbelief of what I was hearing, but in disbelief that I was standing next to the sixth man to walk on the moon. I rarely have had a feeling of awe. I was not standing next to someone who had climbed Mount Everest. I was standing next to one of only a handful of people in the history of our planet who had left it, gone to another celestial body, and returned.

Yet Edgar Mitchell, not just a national celebrity but also a world hero, had that endearing quality which made him a regular guy: he was easy to be with, and easy to talk to.

Surely Susanne had brought a very unique person to the community. And our small group got to hang out with him for a week, to hear anything Edgar felt like talking about.

He told us that being an astronaut was no cakewalk. It was simply gruelling — mentally, emotionally and physically. You'd have to get a PhD or the equivalent at the time, and his was in the mathematics of lunar landings.

On the second morning someone raised his hand and a lively discussion on UFOs began. The comments included the story of how a group of Harvard scientists decided to get to the bottom of the 1947 Roswell incident where the remains of a small alien craft were rumored to have been housed at Wright-Patterson AFB. It seems they had asked themselves a simple question — who would have been immediately sent to Wright Patterson Field if indeed such an incident had been true? Head of the National Security Agency, for example? It turns out the rumor was that travel logs showed they all had gone.

We had a lively discussion about disinformation theory, as practiced by governments not wanting information to be public. In phase one it seems the cognoscenti believe the government denials to be untrue, specifically because the government is denying them. Continual denial as well as no new information characterize phase two. It is a period of doubt. Phase three finds the cognoscenti, still with no new information, dismissing the whole matter and being critical of those who believe it to be true. It is soon swept away from mass consciousness.

So, what really happened at Wright-Patterson Field? We were all left to ponder the issue.

The week was filled with a buzz. Everybody admired, appreciated and enjoyed Edgar. There were those touching moments when he described being in the Houston flight simulator to help guide the malfunctioning Apollo 13 spacecraft home. The entire world listened intently as those astronauts were steered through a harrowing one-minute, two-degree window to safety.

Just as poignant was his epiphany and transformation in space as he looked down on earth from Apollo 14. Edgar explained that at that moment he knew that life in the universe was not just an accident based on random process. For him the epiphany moved him toward a deep desire to become an explorer in the inner realms, the realms of human consciousness.

As a result the Institute of Noetic Sciences was birthed. It is dedicated to research in extended human capacities, integral health and healing, and emerging world views.

Edgar was delighted that one of his friends was there with us. They were working on a consciousness model. While the rest of us were chatting at lunch about more mundane things, you could hear Edgar's brilliant mind jump to high gear. A language of physics and math far beyond my comprehension hovered in the air: they thought consciousness might be similar to a hologram, and with an associate in England were close to mapping it.

I was reminded of being in another hologram: we were in Frank Lloyd Wright's design, transmitted, I am sure, from one of those places Jean Houston would have referred to as "The Essence of Architecture." I wondered what it would be like to be in this space. To Edgar and the other luminaries who came, I am reverently grateful.

*"Who is the happiest of men?
He who values the merits of others,
and in their pleasures takes joy,
even as though 'twere his own."*

Johann Wolfgang Von Goethe

THE KAHUNA LINK, HAWAIIAN SHAMANISM, A CATHOLIC PRIEST AND APPRENTICES TO FRANK LLOYD WRIGHT

Our connections with the Hawaiian community began in earnest when Dr. Hank Wesselman and his wife, Jill Kurdendall, arrived. Hank was a noteworthy paleoanthropologist, college and university professor, and shamanic journeyer. He had spent decades working in the Great Rift Valley with members of the Leakey family and had rubbed elbows with Don Johanson, Lucy's discoverer. They came to give what would turn out to be the first of many popular seminars on shamanism including aspects of the spiritual tradition of the Kahuna mystics of Hawaii.

It was the first night, an open house for the community, and a large crowd showed up at the Frank Lloyd Wright house, curious about what it looked like. Hank related the genesis of his first book, *Spiritwalker*. It seemed he had an uncanny ability to go into extremely deep and altered states. In this state he journeyed some 5,000 years into the future to visit Nainoa, his own future self. The material world we know had long since vanished, reverting back to a more indigenous existence. *Spiritwalker* was the story of Nainoa, the first of a trilogy.

A few minutes into the talk, there was a sudden change in the energy. My hair bristled. I turned slowly around as did everyone else. A large Hawaiian man, walking with a limp and a carrying a large carved staff, entered. He was seven feet tall, and over 300 pounds. At least it felt that way. His graying hair was pulled back into a ponytail. Below his short pants was a large scar, like a battle wound, that dominated one leg. We didn't know it yet, but we would soon learn that this was Hale Makua, not only a Kahuna, but also one of the "Spiritual Elders of all Polynesia." He sat quietly, his face radiating a calming smile as he listened to Hank speak.

For Hank, this appearance was his moment of truth, because much of the material, and his profound knowledge of the Hawaiian language had come to him through direct experience. Was it true? He sensed he was in the presence of not just a Hawaiian elder, but The Big Kahuna.

"Your story's true," he told Hank later.

The link between Makua and Hank blossomed into a powerful association. Makua lectured for an afternoon during this first seminar. We were spellbound! He was a warrior in both the inner and outer worlds.

"They trained me as a Marine 'recon' soldier," he said, "the dangerous stuff. Sent me to Vietnam. I knew it was all about confronting fear."

"Only one way to find out," he laughed. "Stand up in those firefights and make yourself the biggest target possible.

"I'm still here. I've got nine bullet wounds, though. They wanted to take my leg. But I wouldn't let 'em have it."

Makua had a wonderful way of talking about the cosmos and dropping little gems.

"Now is the time for the indigenous people to reveal and share what they know," he said. "We're coming out of the closet."

While almost invisible in Hawaii, he was revered abroad. In New York, while attending a meeting of indigenous elders from around the world he had sat with the Dalai Lama on the stage at the United Nations. Makua's vision was to gather elders from around the world, particularly in Africa, and open a school for them to share what they knew with the world in Hawaii.

When he met with the Voodoo chiefs, he said, "I didn't introduce myself by name. You had to show who you were. The first created spontaneous combustion. Another appeared and disappeared. Yet another turned water into wine."

We never asked Makua what he had demonstrated, but when our dear friend Dr. Ray Rosenthal died, we carried his ashes to Halemaumau, the huge and sacred volcanic caldera on this island. The sky was crystal clear. Makua appeared, larger than life, and began chanting in Hawaiian as part of the ceremony. Suddenly, out of nowhere, the white Messenger Bird appeared circling overhead. When the chant ended, the Messenger Bird disappeared. Perhaps we had witnessed a hint of Makua's powers.

Hank explained that Shamanism was the spiritual practice of virtually all indigenous peoples, predating all of our contemporary organized religions. After the millions of years mankind has been on the earth, Shamanism was, and is, an enduring practice. It was present in virtually all of the indigenous cultures in precisely the same way, revealing the shape of the spiritual worlds; the lower world where one connected with their animal spirit guides; the middle world, or dreamtime, where all sentient beings agreed on their roles in this reality; and the upper world, where one encountered the "teachers."

During the week, drumming ceremonies and numerous guided journeys took us into these worlds. The large carpeted living room and alcove comfortably allowed us to lie down, shut our eyes and let the drumbeats transport us. The house resonated with these ancient practices. Makua observed and encouraged us.

Hank and Jill would be back again and again.

• • •

Our next luminary, Matthew Fox, was an exponent of Creation Spirituality, a movement based on the mystical philosophies springing out of the medieval visions of such people as Hildegard of Bingen, Thomas Aquinas, and Meister Eckhart.

Fox was a pioneer in a spiritual movement stressing the need to find new forms of worship that resonated with the consciousness of younger people. Matthew was intent on blending ideas from Native Americans and technology with traditional forms. The "techno mass" was a current creation of his.

He had just had of one of the most challenging years of his life founding the University of Creation and Spirituality in Oakland. Matthew had previously been excommunicated from the Catholic church over his new ideas. As a Dominican priest, he had disagreed with the Vatican.

"Even Adolf Hitler had avoided excommunication," Matthew said. It had been a tough year.

He was stressed when he arrived, but by the end of week the group, the house, and the Hawaii experience had returned Matthew to a sense of equilibrium.

Finally, our dear friends John and Kay Rattenbury conducted a weeklong seminar on living with Frank Lloyd Wright. It was wonderful to have them there, as they had both been so intimately involved in the construction of this house. John had prepared the working drawings and provided steady guidance from them. Kay had selected colors, fabrics and the interior décor.

Both of them had been part of the Taliesin Fellowship and America's architectural history for over 50 years. The Fellowship was essentially a large family, practicing a method of inner development involving body, mind, and emotions simultaneously. In this sense it seems Taliesin was a conscious community with the art of life as its reason for being. Wright's apprentices had come to be part of a family, as well as practitioners of architecture. It was an atmosphere that celebrated life. Everyone learned by doing, working at whatever needed to be done at the moment.

It was a treat to have them articulate Mr. Wright's principles of Organic Architecture as expressed in this house. Somehow, they infused their own "mana" into the home, with their love of Mr. and Mrs. Wright, Hawaii, and this house. We could feel their joy, and it was timely, as Kay passed away later on in that year.

*"Don't grieve.
Anything you lose
comes round
in another form."*

Rumi

The Energy of the House Raises the Ante

The property needed to be fully landscaped. Windy and dry, the land demanded attention. Fortunately there was an old "awai" system of pasture irrigation ditches providing water when the seasonal stream ran. Years ago, a small group of us had installed irrigation pipes and planted windbreak trees. In the course of shaping the house site, dirt and rock had been artfully deposited, forming a horseshoe berm covering about a half an acre. It was now time for me to get into full-time planting.

Susanne remained unhappy. While the seminars produced rich personal experiences, the money was marginal, and she found that certain of her marketing ideas did not work. We invited friends to attend, at no charge, if there was room.

"If it is all such a good idea, why isn't the universe supporting these seminars?" she lamented. "Why so much resistance?"

I couldn't understand her inner conflicts: they were a "Pandora's box." I didn't want to open it, hoping she would mellow in time. Somehow we were both living with the combined energy of Madam Pele and Frank Lloyd Wright. She took up various activities, hoping to find satisfaction. Jackie Pung, the famous Hawaiian golfer, gave her lessons. That didn't work. Nor did anything else.

While we were "in it" together, we didn't have the same result. My dreams were being fulfilled. The art project had been completed. At some deep and distant place, my Invisible Partners and I were celebrating. I felt well and content, and the sheer delight of the wonderful and unusual people funneling through this portal was exhilarating. Financial losses were marginal and well worth it. I was happy to pay them.

Yet for Susanne, there was no such joy, no such shared feeling of accomplishment. She focused almost entirely on the failing economics of the situation and the nurturing qualities of the city life she so missed. And worse, she saw me enjoying our rural life on the island. She saw me as completely happy, never wanting to return to Honolulu.

Compounding the problem, the advertising agency had come under severe strain. Don's wife had decided to leave both the agency and him. With them together, I felt the agency had a chance. It could have overcome most difficulties. Lynne had been the client service light. They loved her, and so did the staff of the agency. An island girl in her forties, she was a bundle of creative energy with a genuine interest in seeing everyone being rewarded with a win-win. During the competitive presentation for the state McDonald's account, one of the franchises questioned her on the pitfalls of having a husband and wife team. She had studied founder Ray Kroc's book, *Grinding It Out: The Making of McDonald's*. Turning to the gentleman, holding up his book for all to see, she said, "You are so right to be concerned about this, except your own founder relied on husband and wife teams to build the individual franchises throughout America. If you award us the account, rest assured I'll be pumping ketchup through my veins 24/7."

The review committee clapped. I think we won the account at that very moment. She just exuded enthusiasm, connecting the essential umbilical cord between client and agency. But warmth and fuzziness were not Don's strengths. He was admired for his marketing skill, but not his warmth. He needed her. But somehow he had lost his own ability to appreciate how vital she was. On his own, the wheels came off.

Sheraton, the agency's largest account, bid farewell. So did Foodland, then the Prince Hotel chain. As accounts peeled off, Don reached out desperately for new ideas, people, anything. I was asked to come back to help out where I could, even though inwardly I knew it was too late. Commuting back and forth for six months between the islands was exhausting. In the final days, our consultant, Scott Smith, from Tampa, came back to help administer the last rites. We closed the agency, bought out our lease, paid our debts, and hoped loyal employees could receive a small farewell payout. My buyout payments were cut short, a casualty of the collapsing enterprise.

I knew that both Susanne and I were living on frayed nerve ends. We were invited to a wonderful dinner party on the beach. "Dinner and cocktails at Bill and Linda's," read the invitation. They had a beautiful home on one of Hawaii's most treasured strips of white sand. Fine wine and food were guaranteed. More importantly I was looking forward to reconnecting with Susanne, somehow reaching out to find a way to reconstruct the magic we once had.

On the outside, I was cheerful as we walked through the front door, exchanging pleasantries. Inside, the pain was raging. Twenty-five years of hard work, anxiety, failures and adrenalin rushes. The family was dying, and I wasn't good at grief: I knew I could be distant, but it hurt. The horses that were drawing and quartering me were tired, and Susanne and I needed a rest.

That night her radiance was spellbinding. She was no ordinary creature, but gorgeous and charismatic, the mythic warrior princess. After twelve years, we held hands as if we were extensions of the same soul. How lucky could I be to have such a powerful woman by my side.

That usual small talk dominated the dinner, the kind I had grown tired of: real estate, the stock market, and who did what to whom. We headed for the porch during coffee and dessert, to visit alone.

The rocking chair and pounding surf calmed me as I finished that last bite of sweetness. Susanne reached over, gently took my hand and said, "I have something to tell you." Quietly the words rolled off her lips. "I'm having an affair."

Silence.

I did not hear that.

She didn't say that. Yes she did; it was over. It couldn't be. Not that soon. No, it was too early. My insides collapsed. I wasn't ready for it, not then, not ever. I gazed at her, not with anger, but with all the compassion I could muster for myself.

Quietly nodding my head, I said, "Yes, I know."

Where did those words come from? I was remarkably calm. A protective blanket of endorphins settled over me. My guardian angels steadied me.

"I'm in love. I can't help it; I didn't seek it out," she said. "It just happened. I've been swept away, but I didn't go out looking for this feeling; it just ambushed me. If it ever happens to you, you'll know what I mean. I'm happy in our marriage, and I love you both."

The words kept coming, but they were just words now. My eyes were open, and my heart, but I was fading. I couldn't feel anything, and was numb. Something else was operating me. A gentle loving hand reached out and took mine. It was time to go. The party was over.

I stayed in bed for a week, and I told Susanne I was in the love hospital. I didn't want to see anyone. Psychic wounds take time to heal. Deep inside I was hoping that maybe it would play itself out. The island had been difficult, and perhaps this was my penance for having brought her here.

Was I being asked at my core to understand acceptance and non-judgment? I thought so.

Before, these were intellectual topics to bandy about. My face said to the world I was OK, but inside I felt poisoned.

As 1998 ended, I went for a routine physical. There were some elevated test results, and they wanted to poke some holes in my prostate to see if there was anything to be concerned about.

I only heard the doctor's last few words over the phone.

"Mr. Sims, sorry to have to tell you this at Christmas time, but you've got prostate cancer. You've got a little time to think about it, but I wouldn't let this go untreated too long. With surgery or radiation, we are talking about a cure. Otherwise..."

I hung up. The tidal wave of the news hit, and I panicked.

"Get a grip," I told myself. "It's not only what's happening to me, but what I'm going to do about it." Then a stillness descended over me, as if my Invisible Partners had given me a tranquilizing injection.

I had to heal myself on a number of levels.

The energy of the Frank Lloyd Wright home, I reminded myself, was what I had wanted to experience. What would living in the space designed by a mystical genius really be like? One resounding word echoed through my mind: intensity. The inner and outer worlds had been fully engaged. The positives were exhilarating. The negatives were exhausting.

I was caught up in a desire to experience the rich architecture of a genius. Yet there was also a metaphor: a far richer architecture on the drawing boards of my inner world was struggling to emerge, to reveal to me a new design of being. Susanne was on the same journey, pushing, shoving, wrestling, to find peace of mind and new direction.

I was in the rapids of my mind, taking in water, being banged around, paddling desperately to stay afloat and remain right side up. Born out of the churning foam was one idea that slowly emerged, clarified and crystallized: "Make inner peace my top goal." I wanted to feel healthy, happy, joyful and peaceful. All else was just a means of getting there.

I intended to reach calm waters and solid ground.

I saw several doctors who each wanted to treat or cure me with their specialty, but thank God for the Internet, where loads of information was available. I needed a strategy.

Slowly, with a few doctor friends, a strategy emerged.

I tried to do everything to increase my immune system's capability. Time was an ally, and breakthroughs were happening daily. My Gleason score, the measure of a cancer's aggressiveness, was a low 4; not bad. My PSA numbers were single digit. I realized the disease probably would not kill me, at least not tomorrow, if I did my part. I saw that some naturopaths were successfully holding cancer at bay, and reversing it.

I needed to shrink my prostate with hormones, get off alcohol, fat, and sugar, and get in shape. I planned to get an annual MRI/MRSI scan at the University of California to keep tabs on my condition. The plan began to take shape, and the more it did, the stronger, more confident I became.

I told my urologist, the one who called me with the original news, that I had decided to take Androcur, a hormone drug for a year; the drug was meant to shrink my prostate down to nothing.

"The latest *Scientific American* has an article showing that 35 to 40 percent of prostectomies are failures," I told him.

A week later, his letter arrived.

"You're making a big mistake," jumped right off the page, punching me in the stomach.

I told Susanne, "You are not responsible for my cancer. Let's not have that issue plague either of us."

We both realized after reading *The Future of Love* and *Coming Apart* by Daphne Rose Kingma that perhaps our reason for being together had come to an end. The therapy sessions fizzled. We looked at polyamory as a last gasp possibility. I searched Wikipedia and lots of information on multi-partner relationships came up. Susanne urged me to go with her to a local Honolulu polyamory group meeting, but I was still numb and stiff over all of this. Yet something in me wanted desperately to be available, and to look, and to consider. I wanted to be open to something entirely new; I went.

The house was rundown and needed a paint job. The dingy, moldy furniture echoed the energy level of the eight or so people there, and the discussion left us both with a hollow feeling, as if it were a group that hadn't found what it hoped to be. Susanne was still undaunted, until she revealed a dream to me, and her subsequent meeting with a psychic.

"I was walking on a long stretch of gentle beach," she said. "In the distance I saw Jim. He was coming toward me, hand in hand with a beautiful woman. We met.

"'Hi Susanne,' he said, reaching over and giving me a peck on the cheek.

"'I want you to meet Rebecca.'

"The psychic asked me. 'How do you feel at this moment?'

"'Well, I accepted it,' I said. 'I mean yes, I understand that we are living in a polyamorous world…'

"'No, That's not what I asked you,' the psychic pressed. 'I want to know how you feel about Jim and Rebecca.'

"'Jealous! Hurt! Confused,' I said.

"'So, you don't really want to share Jim, do you?' the psychic said. 'Intellectually you think you might like the idea, but emotionally you aren't polyamorous at all.'"

I appreciated Susanne for being real about her feelings, not that they held out any hope for me. Maybe polyamory could work. If it did, one thing was evident: both partners had to be emotionally on the same footing.

And did that really happen? If three or four people all felt exactly the same way about each other, then perhaps. But didn't one person always hold a bit more fascination than another, and how did the balance remain? Maybe it could. I didn't know. Not yet, anyway.

Our heads had tried but our hearts weren't into that, either. At some core level, beyond our intellect, we knew this cycle was over. Marriage, I had heard, was the yoga of the Western World, something you stuck with no matter what, till death did you part. Yet, what was death? Was it physical death, or the end of a joint journey? While our culture had a lot to say about this, we both understood that the only real answer came from deep inside. In those moments of true knowing, not hindered by fear, we must let unconditional love say what it has to say.

Susanne prepared our divorce ceremony based on ideas from Marianne Williamson, a celebrated New Thought spokeswoman. Charlie Campbell, the best man at our marriage ceremony, was the best man at our divorce ceremony. Our goal was to search for a gracious ending. Beginnings are the fun part; endings, how different! Betrayal for me and guilt for her were the primary toxins, and they needed to go, as quickly as possible, for both sanity and physical well-being. I knew it would be slow for me, yet, in those closings moments of that dear chapter of my life I had an epiphany; I now truly understood that when I could forgive, it was not about anyone else. It was about me. It was about my health, and well-being.

"Susanne, I forgive you."

The gathering of close friends took place on the lawn of the Frank Lloyd Wright house. Waves of intense sadness, relief, optimism and joy, coursed through all of us. We laughed, then cried, laughed a little bit more, cried a bit more. We were in new territory.

"How often I found where I should be going only by setting out for somewhere else."

R. Buckminster Fuller

REFLECTIONS

Beginnings are often the grist for joy, happiness and hope. They are the springtime. They are visions of what the seed will produce. They are new friends, new ideas, new adventures. The energy is often youthful, strong, full of life. Beginnings can also be daunting, challenging, and stressful as a portal to the unknown. Frank Lloyd Wright referred to architecture as the highest form of art, perhaps not just because of its appeal to our senses, but to the deeper and richer meaning of mastery. We are all on a journey of mastery. We are the architects of our lives. These journeys are a continuous quest for enriching experiences that leave us wiser at the end than at the beginning. Along the way there are demons and angels, ecstasy and abominations, challenges and accomplishments. At the end we are more seasoned, more capable.

Physically the house was a masterpiece, not only of design, but building. Superb craftsmen were available when they were needed. John had given their work an A+. The exquisite Hawaii site and views far exceeded that of the original location in Pennsylvania. Money showed up well ahead of its need. Had the house's consciousness built itself? Was it not carrying out a truly rich agenda? It would be easy to argue and easy to accept that "other forces" were at work.

Caretakers live lightly. In that regard Susanne and I lived there for less than two years. But you wouldn't have known it. Furnished to serve as a showplace, the house contained unmistakable reproductions of chairs, tables, lamps, hassocks and sofas Wright had created during his lifetime. From the day the house was completed, doors opened to a continuous stream of friends, neighbors, luminaries, seminar attendees, and architectural enthusiasts. Astronauts, kahunas, teachers, artists, explorers, musicians, and scientists all entered. It was a magical portal promoting inspiration, creation, learning and teaching. A rich dialogue was constantly going on.

I remember one night's dialogue on the nature of heaven. Several guests were gathered around the dining room table, keen to push this idea to its limits.

Voice One said, "We all know that heaven is that place where we get anything, anything we want, as soon as we want it. That being the case, wouldn't we eventually arrive at that state where boredom sets in? What then?"

"I agree," Voice Two answered. "If we could instantly gratify ourselves, it would become boring. We'd need an offset, a challenge, an antidote to boredom."

Voice Three said, "Yeah, yeah, a challenge. We'd want to make it more interesting. Not so easy; more like a game."

"OK, I can buy that," Voice One replied. "Then the game would get progressively more refined, complex. Perhaps so difficult nobody could figure it out."

Laughter filled the space. Voice Four smiled and said. "I guess we're in heaven, then. Who's got the corkscrew?"

I thought about that conversation many times, especially as this part of our lives closed. It was time for another ending. The seminars were over, and the marriage was over. The house was complete and I was grieving, but not empty. "Is this state of being really part of heaven?" I asked myself. Maybe in a heaven of challenges it was. Endings are something I was learning about. Our culture is not good at endings.

Even though I needed to sell the house, I could feel my father's hand, as if he had joined my Invisible Partners, patting me on the back for having taken us both on my life's journey. I could feel him relaxing knowing that together we had followed our ancestral DNA impulse to push out into the unknown. Dad had failed to follow his impulse to be a journalist, and done all in his power to encourage me not to make the same decision. While the journey to that point had been laced with challenges, I felt vitally alive for having taken them. I measured rewards not in money, but in facing fear, learning how to accept, understand, forgive. I realized that it wasn't what happened to us, but how we responded – that we have power if we can believe we do. These were the gifts that had come my way and added joy to my soul.

*"It's not the towering sail,
but the unseen wind
that moves the ship."*

Proverb

THE HOUSE GOES UP FOR SALE

It was time to place the house on the market. As the focus home, it was always understood by Taliesin that it would be sold. One of the elements that made the collection of Frank Lloyd Wright designs such an intriguing idea was that nobody really knew what the synergistic value of the collection would be. A stand-alone Frank Lloyd Wright design took on more value the closer it was to a city. Our house was in a rural area, and clearly the most expensive house in this subdivision. These things were working against us. Furthermore, the house was priced at $2.5 million. Buyers in that range often wanted to build their own ideas, and most resort homes were in the compounds on the coast. They were easy to leave, because the resort managed their rental and upkeep. If that were the lifestyle of our buyers they would need to line up caretakers in their absence; not easy.

We listed the house with a firm connected to Sotheby's, looking for international exposure. I feared that Dodie MacArthur, our realtor, would find the house too challenging. How would she tell real buyers from those just wanting a free tour of an architecturally significant home? She said optimistically, "The house has to be show-quality at a moment's notice. You can't live there." OK; out Susanne and I went. The cottages were both ready: one for Susanne, the other for me. The emotional demons were still with me. Her living next door was forcing me to embrace the acceptance and forgiveness that I claimed, especially when her new lover showed up. It was a difficult pill to swallow, but it did go down a bit easier as the days went by.

We got publicity. *The Wall Street Journal* ran a short story. *Extreme Homes* produced a television special, and various magazines featured this late bloom of the genius. All of the correct moves were being made.

Eight months passed with no offers. People were enthusiastically passing through, but there were no buyers.

It was time for a new strategy.

I was in Europe traveling with a doctor friend, Ray Rosenthal. Miraculously cured in three weeks of Non-Hodgkin's Lymphoma the year before, Ray was returning to promote his doctor. We were the perfect odd couple. I was relaxed, and taking it all in. Ray was a type A Jewish perpetual motion machine with a big heart. He had to shower two, maybe three times a night, just to calm down.

"I became an emergency room doc to relax," he quipped one day. "I don't know what it is, but in that chaotic environment I find myself at peace, like being in the eye of a storm," he said.

Bonn, Germany, where Ray's doctor lived, was our home base for the summer. I was anxious to take a few days from there to see Dr. Franz Lutz at the Institute of Resonance Therapy, in Cappenberg, not far away. Carol Wong, an artist friend of both Susanne's and mine, had made the suggestion before I left. She had called and said, "I'll contact Franz for you. He's a medical doctor experimenting with energetics in a new way. I worked there a year in his laboratory. Go see him. His mother is a well-known faith healer, a mistress to Count Kanetz. The institute is on the Count's castle grounds. In fact he is underwriting the whole thing. You'll go for what Franz does, I promise. I won't say anymore right now, except that it will be, well…" She paused and smiled. "Out of the box stuff. You know, the kind you go for," she said.

As surviving cancer patients we were first headed for a nine-day seminar at Lake Orta, Italy, with Faisal Muqqudam. Faisal was a co-developer of the "Diamond Approach," and Ridwan School in Berkeley, California. The seminar was on the "Nature of Love." Mostly experiential, lots of professional therapists and long time followers of Faisal, including Ray, would attend. I was being allowed in, perhaps as courtesy to Ray. Anything that could help promote and maintain self-healing was valuable to me. I was happy to tag along, but I had a habit of purposely treating these trips rather naively at first. From there it was on to Bonn. Ray secretly wanted several interviews with his doctor, the famous Wolfgang Scheef, hoping to nominate him for the Nobel Prize in Alternative Medicine. I really cheered for Ray, for he had the energy and the brain power if he could stay focused.

We pulled into the Bonn train station and grabbed our bags, hurrying to hail a taxi for the clinic. A pleasant juxtaposition of old buildings festooned with flower-boxed windows flew by in a blur. I guess the cabbie really sensed Ray's eagerness. Then, on a tree-lined street, passing the residence of Beethoven, I couldn't help but think, "We're in the genius energy now." The streets were filled with smiling faces enjoying the blessings of the long daylight and warm weather of summer. Ray tapped the driver frantically. We stopped and backed up. Ray bounded up the step of the drab Janker Clinic building, bags in hand, to an open door he knew so well. Peeking into Dr. Scheef's office, we seized the moment and barged in. He saw us from the corner of his eye and a big smile crossed his face.

"Ray, Ray! Come in, come in." He jumped out of his chair to give Ray a big hug. Standing before me was one of medicine's heroic figures. Ray whispered to me under his breath, "He speaks six languages including, get this, Latin. He's a concert pianist, has an M.D., and Ph. Ds in both pharmacology and history. He gave himself a melanoma just to test his own vaccine, and he also invented a technique of low-dose radiation to crack cancer cells, coupled with one mega hit of chemotherapy. It was never approved by the German FDA, but so what? So many prominent people, like those in the Bundestag, were saved that nobody dared to touch him. He did it to me. One big blast. Of course it took a year to recover. But no more big C, and good-bye twelve pound tumor."

They both had so much to tell and share with each other. The air was electric. Somehow Ray's complete surrender to Dr. Scheef had exceeded the doctor-patient bond. There was a compassionate connection between them that embodied the richest experience of being a human being, the kind we all yearn for. After a few minutes, while both seemed to be taking a breather, the doctor turned to me, as if I were now one of the family. He grabbed my large envelope, quickly raised each film to the window light, and mumbled to himself in German. Then with eyes that radiated more warmth and compassion than I had ever felt from any doctor, I heard, "Sandy, I have seen over 250,000 cancer patients in my life. I can promise you that you will never ever die from this disease. Come on, the day is over. Let's all go have a beer."

Coming from such an authority figure, any doubts or lingering concerns instantly melted into the thought of how joyously I was going to enjoy that beer. Maybe two!

Still vibrating from his comments, I wondered to myself. "Was this not a meeting helped or arranged by my Invisible Partners? Yes!" I finally understood. They got full credit. And furthermore, I resolved that they would also get full credit for any future good fortune coming my way. Even with setbacks, they had my best interests at heart. Perhaps our glitches are simply catalysts for something more rewarding around the corner.

The next weekend Ray and I visited the Institute of Resonance Therapy.

*"At first people refuse to believe
that a strange new thing can be done,
then they begin to hope it can be done,
then they see it can be done —
then it is done, and all the world wonders why
it was not done centuries ago."*

Frances Hodgson Burnett

Courtesy Carolyn Blake Photography

Entering A New World

Franz pulled up in an aging cream colored Mercedes. In no time Ray and Franz were into "Doc talk." I sat quietly, as the car pulled into a long, narrow, cobblestoned driveway. We entered the manicured grounds of the castle, located on a hundred or so acres. You could see the lake below, and I was looking for deer. The landscape felt unusually alive and healthy. Franz said, "This was one of the first projects IRT undertook." Then, in front of us loomed the massive castle compound. "There must be 100 rooms or more. I've only been in half them myself," Franz said.

The car pulled up to our quarters, a brand new addition that blended modern glass, halogen lights, and hardwood floors with ancient stone and brick. Franz gave us a tour of the state-of-the-art auditorium used for high-level symposiums. We stowed our bags and walked down to a stand-alone stone building, the laboratory. Inside were rows of radionic machines and time sequenced pictures showing the improved conditions of forests and farms under treatment.

We learned that IRT had been dedicated to harnessing and balancing other energy fields to affect the health of all kinds of systems. A system, in this sense, could include anything from land, to buildings, to plants, to animals: even people. The energy fields were comprised of oranur, orgone and dor as described by Wilhelm Reich, the controversial Austrian-American psychiatrist.

Definitely ahead of their time, IRT had pioneered techniques using radionics to clear away harmful energy patterns, mostly on European farms and forests, to increase growth and attract conditions that before were blocked. The walls of the laboratory were lined with before and after treatment pictures of specific locations.

Hale Makua, the Kahuna Hawaiian Chief on the Big Island, had made me aware that the Frank Lloyd Wright house sat smack dab in the middle of battlefields where long ago, dreadful amounts of blood had been spilled. Warriors who arrived by canoe to the beaches some ten miles or so down below, slowly fought their way up the mountain to Waimea. Franz told me this energy could be cleared.

"Applying our treatment from here, we can make your house and land much more attractive energetically," Franz said.

Carol was right. I was attracted to Franz's work and thinking. Ray nodded, and we both recognized that Franz was on to something. The M.D. in his title appealed to my conservative linear mind; the part of me that was comfortable, wanted to rule, was on familiar turf. He quoted me a price; $6,000. Once I would have balked. The ideas would have been intriguing, but the money would have stopped me. Now it was easier, I felt more tuned in. I accepted that not all of the work of my Invisible Partners had to be a dramatic, cataclysmic struggle. Certain synchronicities and intuitive hits became second nature, and Franz's approach would connect to a new resonating pattern.

Years before, I had attended an annual meeting of our ad agency network, World Wide Partners. Some 100 agencies from around the globe met semi-annually to network and share ideas. The guest speaker at one of these meetings divided us into groups of four or five. Our assignment: list twenty good ideas for marketing a specific project. Since this was our expertise, we attacked the assignment. After fifteen minutes, he said, "Throw away fifteen of those ideas." We debated, cajoled, disagreed, and finally whittled them down to the top five.

Then he said, to groans and moans, "Now, throw away the remaining five ideas and start the assignment. You cannot use any, let me repeat, any of the twenty ideas."

The purpose of the exercise was to encourage us to reach inaccessible ideas. Jewels like these frequently languish, because people limit themselves to their initial inspirations. Although your first ideas may be good, refusing to go further limits the potential for an epiphany.

Franz's approach could yield just such a gem. I had been spending money on advertising, publicity resources, and all the right things most rational people would do. Yet, no results. Why not sign up for something completely different? Even the rational side of my brain was starting to agree.

The fundamental idea of radionics was developed by Albert Abrams, a controversial California medical doctor and Stanford professor, in the early twentieth century. He observed that a healthy person possessed certain frequencies that represent health. Conversely, an unhealthy person will exhibit different frequencies. The radionic device sends the healthy frequency to replace the discordant frequency in the sick person.

Ruth Drown, a physician, discovered that Abrams' treatment could also work at a distance. From a drop of blood sent in the mail she diagnosed and treated patients. The blood droplet was referred to as a resonator. Because radio waves were believed to be involved the method was called radionics. Later an engineer, Curtis Upton, applied the idea to other living creatures and plants.

Franz's mother, Irene, picked up on this thinking and renamed the methodology resonance therapy because it had been determined that there was an unknown resonance involved other than radio waves. Rupert Sheldrake, an English biologist, has called the phenomenon morphic resonance, and the field in which it occurs the Morphogenetic field.

Our goal was to measure the energetics thrown off by the Frank Lloyd Wright house and the immediate surrounding land. If it was low, referred to as "dor" or "stuck energy" in Reichian terms, we would need to raise it. If it was high, called "oranur," the "frenetic energy," we would need to calm it. The goal would be to transpose "dor" and "oranur" to "orgone," the balanced state. The roughly 3.5 acres and house were the area to be treated, referred to as the "holon."

On my return from Europe, I obtained spring water, placed it in small unused bottles, and left them in the house for three days. We gathered soil specimens, as well as photographs of the house and grounds. All of these samples were termed "resonators." That is, they contained information about the whole, just as a cell in the body exhibits the entire body's blueprint. Because they contained this information they were also called "attractors." Morphic fields and attractors have no boundaries.

Franz analyzed the energetic patterns of the soil and water samples using a copper chloride crystallization method to establish a base line. He used the radionics machine attached to an "orgone shooter," (a small device looking like a miniature rocket about to launch) to treat the property and measure the change in energy.

The initial assessment of the energy levels was that they were 21 percent of what they should be. There was both stagnating dor energy, perhaps from the battlefields, and hyperactive oranur energy caused by the volcanoes. The impression was that the negative energies could be transformed, and the positive energies built up.

The ideal energetic level is measured in a unit called the "Bovis." Antoine Bovis was a French physicist who, in the '30s, developed a life-energy measuring scale. For living organisms the key reference is 6,500. Below this, a charge is life-detracting. Above this, it is life-enhancing. The ideal range for humans is between 8,000 to 10,000 energy units. The earth generates energy in the 7,000 to 18,000 range, a positive radiation necessary for sustaining life.

Franz didn't believe that the house should go beyond 8,000 Bovis. He said, "I see the potential of the structure not so much as a holy place but more as a site of high life energy. That's what you need to solve very practical problems."

A cathedral might have a Bovis rating at the 13,000 or 14,000 level, a little too much as a steady diet for ordinary mortals.

This seemed quite true. I have wandered into the large monumental cathedrals of Europe, only to start telling myself after a half an hour or so, "Enough. It's time to go."

The next part of the process was finding information that the system could use to solve the problem for itself. This type of information was stored in resonating patterns. The key would be to find patterns that resonated with the system's attractors. These were called "informators."

IRT kept a wide range of Hebrew symbols, pictures of dolphins, crop circles, Mandelbrot sets (a set of points in the complex plane, the boundary of which forms a fractal) — in short, a variety of pictograms. A pendulum would be passed over these pictograms until one or more gave a strong energetic response.

Both the informatory symbol and the attractor (in our case the soil sample and the water crystallization pattern) were inserted into the radionics machine. Our house faced south-southwest, forming a critical rotation point capable of picking up the transmissions.

Over the next several months there was a definite change in the crystallization patterns of the water. These were photographed and sent to me, indicating that we were achieving our objectives.

I was now more curious than ever about the nature of any potential buyer.

Toward the end of the treatment the first person, Charles, a California man, appeared. He flew out for only one day. An engaging man, Charles was of moderate height, perhaps in his late forties. Rounds of plastic surgery hid the effects of a horrible auto accident. Shouldering a large briefcase, much like the ones in which pilots carry all the pertinent details of their aircraft, Charles regaled us with his numerous projects. He was even bidding for the failed Motorola Iridium Satellite project. Yet we were a bit perplexed. Charles didn't seem to want the usual details one might expect. Dodie, my realtor, and I exchanged those "What gives?" looks. Finally he told us that he had made up his mind the moment he saw the house. On further inquiry we found that he wanted to use the house in a way that would violate subdivision covenants. Not wanting to see either of us disappointed (as I would be carrying a note for some time), I turned down his offer. However, we were now getting activity. The morphogenetic field had been stimulated.

Shortly thereafter, while I was in New Zealand, Dodie emailed me.

"Got another one who wants to buy your house, but he doesn't have any money. At least not now. He wants to make a proposal when you return."

Where were these people coming from? Something new was happening.

"I think I'll be quiet on this one," I said to myself.

I liked Robert Lynch from the moment I met him. He was authentic, straightforward and had a dry sense of humor. He was delightful. Robert was on vacation with his wife, Jennifer, and was staying at the Mauni Lani Bay Resort. It was just down the hill a few miles. They saw a picture of the house, and contacted Dodie.

Robert told me, "I planned to purchase a home next year, but spirit guided me to this home. It's meant for me, and all there is left to do is take care of the details."

When he said that spirit had guided him, I knew he was the right person, because many people might have felt like this but few would have said it.

Robert, Rick and I met in Rick's office to review the proposal. We learned that Robert had been a founder of Harmony Foods, years ago. He had sold the thousand-employee company not too many years later. After that, he diversified into real estate development, brine shrimp farming, and specialized food products.

Robert's offer! No money down. I realized it was a fair enough price, at $2 million, and it could work. Robert was willing to begin making monthly payments on a lease-to-purchase basis, pending title and other subdivision clarifications. In no time Rick drew up a contract. It gave Robert and Jennifer the house they loved, down to the silverware. Four months later, Robert gave me more than he had agreed to: a check for half the sales price.

The long walk down their driveway felt good. Robert and Jennifer were regularly asking me to give the "official tour" to visitors and friends. We became fast friends.

Anything you've been good at often becomes addictive. Business is no exception. Before long Robert found an opportunity with a former business partner, Ron Koenig. They started a company called Viack. Their state-of-the-art software made online meetings virtually impregnable to outsiders. Others were offering the same service, but Viack's technology was light-years ahead. Marketing and distribution were the challenges. In no time they ramped up to some 80 or so employees. Knowing my background in advertising and marketing Robert asked me to join Viack's marketing advisory board, and I was honored. In almost the same breath, he offered to sell me the stock and options of two employees who were leaving the company.

"Sandy, I think this investment will return to you the price of your house fourfold... in time."

I thought about what losing the money would feel like. Like selling the house for less. Did I need the money? No. But would I have liked to have it? Yes! Would I be able to live with the loss? Yes, but my ego wouldn't like it. I bought the stock and options. Billy and Hans each received 20,000 shares of the company. I hoped it would turn out well, a possible dividend from the house. Were my Invisible Partners involved in this decision? I wanted to say yes. On second thought, their message was more like, "Of course we're here, but you can handle this one on your own. You're getting stronger now."

"Wisdom begins in wonder."

Socrates

Courtesy Carolyn Blake Photography

The Road Ahead

The Hawaii Collection has not emerged, but it still may. Yet, it has been a wonderfully rich adventure. My partners, the people whom I have met, and the special homes and buildings I have been privileged to experience have all been a wonderful part of my life's adventure. Art and beauty have been transformative to my soul. The awareness of how the Fellowship of the Frank Lloyd Wright Foundation made their lives a conscious art form profoundly influenced me. Was I tested? Yes, but without the stretch there couldn't have been this adventure. My enduring question has been, "Are there Invisible Partners who step forward to help us on our journey?" If the motive is pure experience; yes, I am convinced there are. And the more they are recognized, the more frequently they appear. Money from the architectural commission of the clubhouse had showed up at a critical time for the Foundation. That was a blessing. Was the money needed by the Foundation really the purpose of the Hawaii Collection? I can't say. If so, the entire experience from that moment on was a resounding success.

The return on investment in Robert's company has yet to materialize. We will see.

As for the house, I had naively gone forth for the pure experience of building this marvelous house and finding out what its energy might have in store for me, and it revealed itself to have been a portal. At times, it seemed to have built itself. The way money arrived, the events that took place, and the people who showed up were extraordinary.

As for the energy of being in the house, there was a profound intensity at all times: when easy, it was exhilarating, when challenging, it made me a better human being. My marriage dissolved, yet I learned acceptance and non-judgment. If my life were to end tomorrow, those two realizations would have made the journey worthwhile.

Frank Lloyd Wright was a Great Soul, and my life's journey has been enriched by the sweep of his cosmic influence on me.

We are all architects of our life's design. If our creations can enhance our experience and add to future experiences, life will be a journey well worth the taking.

As on any wonderful trip, we enjoy the people whom we have met and those who help make the trip possible, whether we come face-to-face with them or not. If we realize that our Invisible Partners travel with us constantly, we can continuously turn the ordinary into the wonder of the extraordinary.

*"There are only two ways to live your life.
One is as though nothing is a miracle. The
other is as though everything is a miracle."*

Albert Einstein

Courtesy Carolyn Blake Photography

Epilogue

People might say, "What's the big deal? That guy just had an idea, and one thing led to another." Perhaps, but there is another way to look at it. Our antennae can be up and always receiving. We can be tuned into synchronistic developments, and set priorities based on them, taking us down a path that is not random, but has an order. It is a partnership with unseen forces. My involvement with the Frank Lloyd Wright Foundation and what followed came from my becoming aware, and then my willingness to follow through on that awareness.

The Foundation members, of course, had their desires and hopes. While more might have been realized, the large architectural commission could not have come at a better time. Maybe their Invisible Partners were working on their behalf.

"What about the Waikapu Mauka Partners and the Shimizu Corporation? It doesn't look like their dreams and aspirations came to fruition. What about their hopes and desires?"

All of our dreams, goals and intentions are at play in the context of larger forces. Howard sensed that Japan was engaged in a huge economic bubble and wanted to bring the project to the marketplace at a much quicker pace. In the end, great market forces had their way. The opposing forces were so huge when the market collapsed that lesser forces were simply no match. Had the Shimizu company been willing to go to market a bit sooner, homes might have been pre-sold and the project might have moved forward in spite of the severe downturn in the Japanese market. In the ethereal world, maybe there are different rules as to what receives support and what does not.

Some might ask, "What about negative forces such as evil? Could our Invisible Partners or our intuition lead us into harm's way?" Einstein is credited with asking the question, "Is the universe friendly?" All around us there are examples of tragedy. People appear to live along a continuum book-ended by joy and happiness at one extreme and severe pain at the other. There are those suffering at the hands of others and those who suffer in the constructs of their minds. Yet the planets seem to operate in precise orbits, and the chemistry of the earth is perfectly balanced, making life possible.

Years ago I took a comparative religion course in college. The issue of the holocaust arose. Perplexed, students asked why this should happen. The professor, in the way that our culture permitted said, "God works in mysterious ways. You must simply have faith." I sat there thinking to myself, "There has to be a better answer than that." Years later, I began reading Eastern philosophy books. Their answer to the plight of those born into deplorable conditions, or those who encountered misfortune, was karma.

Karma implies that human consciousness continues to grow by moving from one life to the next. The good deeds, thoughts, and ways of being are rewarded in both present and future incarnations. The harmful deeds, thoughts, and behavior results in one's suffering both in present and future lives. There is a cosmic balance constantly in play. Consciousness evolution is a growing awareness of these causes and effects. Empirical evidence seems to support this view, because the vast majority of people inherently know right from wrong, regardless of their life situations.

Had my religion teacher brought up the concept of karma I could have had a rational explanation in place of a mystery: I might have had a more utilitarian concept by which to live. Even if karma did not exist, good behavior, thinking and deeds would be more likely to serve me than the opposite because daily life delivers that evidence.

If I follow my intuition or synchronistic signposts to what appears to be a disaster, does that mean that negative forces have triumphed? Maybe karma is being paid off, and in the future, my perspective will have been broadened to see the gift in what happened.

After each setback there is always a point of choice. What action am I now going to take? My belief is that at any of these points, forces are aligned to help us, and it is our attitude that determines the effectiveness of these efforts. In looking back we can always see the wisdom in the path.

My own experience is that when the purpose is to do something for the sheer joy of it, the universe seems to cooperate. If the goal is to compete and win, then there are opposing forces with opposing desires. A loss may not mean a failure, but may simply prove that an outcome was not in the flow of a larger movement, or that your loss created an opportunity you do not yet see.

We are moving from the driver's seat, with plenty of time to survey the maps and weigh the pros and cons of various routes, to a new dynamic. Time appears to be compressing. No longer is there the luxury of mulling things over. One must simply act, and now there is a need to tap into a deep-seated sense of direction, move in that direction, and trust that the necessary elements will fall into place. To remain sane, we want to see signposts assuring us that we are on course. Our signposts are not just random, but part of a larger force.

You can see this compression of time and the responses to it in business, where companies have gone to horizontal team structures, eliminating middle management. Paper is being eliminated in favor of digital communication, and we have instant access to information via the internet, computers and computerized telephones, all of which push us at a relentless pace. Young people can text two people at one time, with cell phones in both hands, while carrying on a verbal conversation.

How do we adapt to this new frequency while staying in balance and maintaining health? First we acknowledge that this acceleration has happened. Secondly, we consciously gather the tools to adapt ourselves to this dynamic. Think of it as a means of survival; if we resist or do not adapt, forces eventually may create so much upheaval in our lives that health and well-being may go.

I seem to experience both active and passive states. These could be components of the same process. For example where does that original pure urge come from? Who sent it? We all have Invisible Partners. Perhaps they have sent the original urge. But that is unimportant to me; that they are here is all that matters. Often I look for the urge to occur. I meditate and seek answers from many sources, and then wait for a knowing, a connection I feel is there. Once it arrives, my active state says, "This is what my Invisible Partners and I want. I am going to move in that direction even though I don't know the outcome. I am going to use my brain to discern. I am going to look for signs, whether they are synchronistic outer symbols or internal feelings, that I am on the path: not side-tracked, but in touch with my Partners."

Can I stay on course, stay in touch with my Invisible Partners, and make it happen? It's easy to see small accomplishments. All of the elements are identifiable. But cause and effect are likely to go unnoticed. For example, let's say I want to talk to someone. The next thing I know, I've run into them on the street or in a store.

Yet, as a task or goal increases in size, the unknowable element increases. Doubt ensues: so much so in a few cases that, to put it bluntly, I have been very frightened. Faith that it will happen becomes an ordeal. The bigger desires, I have noticed, take longer and seem more likely to occur if the goal is a pure experience. Desiring a lot of money to take care of a basic insecurity may not happen, perhaps because there is a fear of lack. Lack is what really gets transmitted and lack, or nothing, is the result. Furthermore the lag factor may be so great that when the event finally does occur, there is no memory of the original desire. Consequently, no connection is made that your Partners had anything to do with the outcome.

This is where the signposts, the synchronicities, become so important; they are the reassurances I've needed to keep from feeling I was not out of my mind. The small things that occur with no great risk attached are important: they are like springboards to the next level. We don't just dive off the high tower. There is a long slow process of gaining confidence by diving from boards at incrementally greater heights.

Everyone has synchronistic events taking place in their lives daily. For example, you are thinking about calling someone. Suddenly the phone rings. That someone is on the other end of the line. The value of the synchronicity is to consciously recognize it, and harvest the message. Maybe that person called to tell you about an event they thought you ought to attend; that event ought to go to the top of your priority list. You will either meet someone or gather some important information there, on the way, or on the way back. Once you start seeing ordinary life from this perspective, the ordinary can become extra-ordinary. You'll now attend this event with your antennae up, and everyone and everything will become fully alive as you look for the next clue.

As we recognize these signposts our uncertain journey is transmuted into more certainty. We can relax more into the unknown without feeling we are completely lost or doomed. It's not an easy process. It can be quite nerve-wracking, especially as the stakes are raised: like quitting your job to travel for a year, or moving to a new location without having a good reason other than a strong urge. Yet, it is this that begins to create a certainty and validity, one that will eventually give you as much confidence as the linear way we live now. I admit that I waffle back and forth, knowing at some deep level and yet being afraid much of the time to take the plunge.

The most fun is to use the baby-step approach. Practice on things that really don't matter, and give yourself feedback when you recognize the connection.

One useful exercise is to review your life. Pick out those big breaks, turning points, that were referred to as luck, coincidence, or fate. Review these patterns and see if the actions you took were congruent, or if you resisted. Did you go for the action that felt right even though it felt iffy? If so, how did it work out? Or, did you back off and take a safer route? How did that work out? We've all done both, probably over and over. I remember the musical conductor I saw being interviewed on one of the evening talk shows. He was asked what he had learned in life. He answered, "When confronted with a decision, one being difficult the other easy, I always take the tougher one first, because the road gets easier toward the end. If I take the easy road first, it seems more difficult toward the end."

In the more immediate past, we can remember small events where things happened as we wanted. Somebody had a phone number or important piece of information you needed just at that moment. A parking place or elevator opened up for you while you were in a hurry. Or perhaps nothing was going right, suggesting that you were perhaps off course. Yet those delays could also have been for a useful purpose. Maybe you needed to meet someone you didn't know you were going to meet, but you needed to be delayed a bit.

Then there are just nice things that happen with no preconceived desire, thought or awareness. A few summers ago, for example, I was walking down the street in Barcelona. I had a small map in my pocket. As I took it out while walking, my money clip fell on the street. Within moments someone tapped me on the shoulder. Turning around, I gazed into the eyes of a smiling man who presented me with my money. Did this happen for no reason? Was this just a nice honest man? Or were my Invisible Partners involved? I like to think that yes, these are my pals. I can't see them, but we're going though life together, me here, and they in the invisible world.

The Invisible Challenge

Here is my recommendation: it won't be a big investment. Get a small pocket-sized flip-pad dedicated to just this exercise, and each time something comes together — the coincidental meeting, the parking place, the phone call with just the right info — jot it down. If it is a synchronistic event with a useful piece of information, you can act on it. Record this: where did that take you, or is it still taking you? If a big event materializes, note it, trying to remember how long it took to come about. Of course there may just be the "aha" experience. For example I was traveling with Charlie Campbell. We were stopped at a traffic light, and I asked him what time it was. Looking straight ahead at the rear of the car in front of us he read "6PM," boldly printed on the rear license tag of the car in front of us. A quick glance at our watches revealed exactly 6:00 p.m. We both laughed.

As we see the signs, we improve the communication. Events materialize. Our confidence builds. Lastly, if nothing is on your wish list, make happiness and joyfulness a desire. You and your Invisible Partners will enjoy that assignment. Have a wonderful journey.

A BRIEF LIST OF AUTHORS WHO INFLUENCED ME IN MY JOURNEY, AS WELL AS OTHER SUGGESTED READINGS

Alder, Vera Stanley. *Finding of the Third Eye.* San Francisco: Weiser Books, 1980.
—. *Humanity Comes of Age.* Great Britain: Aquarian Press, 1956.
—. *Initiation of the World.* San Francisco: Weiser Books, 2000.
—. *The Fifth Dimension.* San Francisco: Weiser Books, 2000.

Caddy, Eileen. *Flight into Freedom and Beyond: The Autobiography of the Co-Founder of the Findhorn Community.* Forres: Findhorn Press, 2002.

Campbell, Joseph. *Myths to Live By.* London: Souvenir Press Ltd, 1995.
—. *Reflections on the Art of Living: A Joseph Campbell Companion.* New York: Harper Perennial, 1995.
—. *The Hero with a Thousand Faces.* Novato, CA: New World Library, 2008.
—. *The Inner Reaches of Outer Space: Metaphor as Myth and as Religion.* Novato, CA: New World Library, 2002.

Campbell, Joseph, and Bill Moyers. *The Power of Myth.* New York: Anchor, 1991.

Csikszentmihalyi, Mihaly. *Flow: The Psychology of Optimal Experience.* New York: Harper Perennial Modern Classics, 2007.
—. *Finding Flow: The Psychology of Engagement with Everyday Life.* New York: Basic Books, 1997.

Houston, Jean. *A Mythic Life: Learning to Live our Greater Story.* New York: Harperone, 1996.
—. *Jump Time: Shaping Your Future in a World of Radical Change.* Boulder, Colorado: Sentient Publications, 2004.

Jung, C. G. *Synchronicity: An Acausal Connecting Principle.* Princeton: Princeton University Press, 1973.

Kingma, Daphne Rose. *The Future of Love.* San Francisco: Main Street Books, 1999.

Lama, Dalai. *The Art of Happiness, 10th Anniversary Edition: A Handbook for Living.* New York: Riverhead, 2009.

Leonard, George. *Mastery: The Keys to Success and Long-Term Fulfillment.* New York: Plume, 1992.

Ouspensky, P. D. *The Fourth Way.* New York: Vintage, 1971.

Rattenbury, John. *A Living Architecture: Frank Lloyd Wright and Taliesin Architects.* Petaluma: Pomegranate Communications, 2000.

Redfield, James. *The Celestine Prophecy.* New York: Warner Books, 1995.
—. *The Tenth Insight: Holding the Vision.* New York: Warner Books, 1998.

Redfield, James and Carol Adrienne. *The Celestine Prophecy: An Experimental Guide.* New York: Grand Central Publishing, 1995.

Roberts, Jane. *Seth Speaks: The Eternal Validity of the Soul.* San Rafael, CA: Amber-Allen Publishing., New World Library, 1994.
—. *The Nature of Personal Reality: Specific, Practical Techniques for Solving Everyday Problems and Enriching the Life You Know.* San Rafael, CA: Amber-Allen Publishing, New World Library, 1994.

Roberts, Jane, and Seth. *The "Unknown" Reality, Vol. 1: A Seth Book.* San Rafael: Amber-Allen Publishing, 1997.
—. *The "Unknown" Reality, Vol. 2: A Seth Book.* San Rafael: Amber-Allen Publishing, 1997.
—. *The Individual and the Nature of Mass Events. A Seth Book.* San Rafael: Amber-Allen Publishing, 1995.
—. *The Magical Approach: Seth Speaks About the Art of Creative Living.* San Rafael, CA: Amber-Allen Publishing, New World Library, 1995.

Robbins, Anthony. *Awaken the Giant Within: How to Take Immediate Control of Your Mental, Emotional, Physical and Financial Destiny!* New York City: Free Press, 1992.

Russell, Peter. *Waking Up In Time: Finding Inner Peace In Times of Accelerating Change.* Novato: Origin Press, 2007.

Spangler, David. *The Laws of Manifestation: A Consciousness Classic.* San Francisco: Weiser Books, 2009.

Talbot, Michael. *The Holographic Universe.* Harper Perennial, 1992

Wright, Frank Lloyd. *Frank Lloyd Wright: An Autobiography.* Petaluma: Pomegranate Communications, 2005.

Yatri. *Unknown Man: The Mysterious Birth of a New Species.* New York: Fireside, 1988.

A SAMPLING OF THE BOOKS WRITTEN BY LUMINARIES WHO HELD SEMINARS AT THE FRANK LLOYD WRIGHT HOUSE

Edgar, Dwight Williams, and Dr. Edgar Mitchell. *The Way of the Explorer: An Apollo Astronaut's Journey Through the Material and Mystical Worlds.* Franklin Lakes: New Page Books, 2008.

Fox, Matthew. *Creativity.* New York: Tarcher, 2004.
—. *Passion for Creation: The Earth-honoring Spirituality of Meister Eckhart.* New York: Inner Traditions, 2000.
—. *The Reinvention of Work: A New Vision of Livelihood for Our Time.* New York: Harperone, 1995.

Kubby, Steve, and Terence McKenna. *The Politics of Consciousness: A Practical Guide to Personal Freedom.* Port Townsend: Breakout Productions, 1995.

McKenna, Terence. *True Hallucinations: Being an Account of the Author's Extraordinary Adventures in the Devil's Paradise.* New York: Harperone, 1994.

Moody, Raymond A. *The Last Laugh: A New Philosophy of Near-Death Experiences, Apparitions, and the Paranormal.* Charlottesville: Hampton Roads Publishing Company, 1999.
—. *Life After Life: The Investigation of a Phenomenon – Survival of Bodily Death.* San Francisco: Harper San Francisco, 2001.

Wesselman, Hank. *Medicinemaker.* United States and Canada: Bantam, 1999.
—. *Spiritwalker: Messages from the Future.* United States and Canada: Bantam, 1996.
—. *Visionseekers.* Carlsbad: Hay House, 2002.

INDEX

accident on site of Hawaii Island house, 118
ad agency
　final collapse of, 156
　Sandy is bought out of, 121-122
　Sandy returns to, 156
　Sandy's first, 37
　thoughts on starting an, 31
advertising, thoughts on, 15
affair, Sandy's reaction to Susanne's, 158
agency, starting an, 31
Alder, Vera Stanley, 38
Apollo 13, Edgar Mitchell on, 147
art
　and brother, 10
　kinetic vs. static, 96
astronaut training, Edgar Mitchell on, 146
attractors, 177
autobiographies, first experience with, 33
Baney, Tonia, 82
bank, job offer from, 29
bartender, and effect on Sandy, 18-19
Beah, see grandmother,
book, discount, and experiences with, 30
boulder, uncovered, 109
Bovis, 178
brother
　and art, 10
　and club feet, 9
　and Heaven's Gate, 10
　and schizophrenia, 10
business school, 27
buyout of Sandy's ad agency, 121-122
Byington, see brother,
Caddy, Peter, 40-43
Campbell, Charlie, 57, 162, 193
cancer, Sandy's diagnosis with, 158-160
childhood
　in Florida, 5
　and psychological testing, 15
Clement, Frank, 73-74
club feet, and brother, 10
clubhouse for Hawaii Collection, 87-88
coals, hot, walking on, 52-53
college lecturer, offer of job as, 29
college professor, and effect on Sandy, 17-18
Cornwell House, see Hawaii Island house
Creation Spirituality, 151
creative thinking, thoughts on, 189-192
decision-making, thoughts on, 191
desire, thoughts on, 190
Diamond Approach, 170

discount book, experiences creating and marketing, 30
divorce
　of parents, 6
　Sandy's ceremony, 162
　thoughts on, 183
dor, 177-178
doubt, thoughts on, 190
draft, thoughts on, 18
Elfins, 144
eruption of Halemaumau volcano, 26
eschaton, 144
Europe, travels through, 27
exams
　Financial Analysis, 28
　navigation, 24
father, 7
　death of, 115
　holiday luncheon with, 13-14
　and Sandy's decision to move to Hawaii, 11
　watching over Sandy, 166
　and writing, 8
Fellowship, Taliesin, 58, 65
financial talk, and mysterious stranger, 13-14
firewalking, 52-53
Florida, growing up in, 5
focus home
　cost of, 73
　plans for, 73
foundation, options for laying stone, 110
Fox, Matthew, 123, 151
Frank Lloyd Wright Conservancy, 95
Frank Lloyd Wright Foundation, 58, 68
frenetic energy, 177
friend at hotel school, lesson learned from, 20-21
G.R., see grandfather,
Galt, Randolph, 55-56
Georgie, lesson learned from, 20-21
God, thoughts on, 78
golf courses
　construction of, 91
　plans for, 83
graduation from OCS, 24
grandfather
　and New Port Richey, 6
　impact on Sandy's childhood, 7
grandmother, memories of, 7-8
Griswold, and Financial Analysis course, 27-28
Groark, John, 133

Gwynn, Billy, 106-107
Hacienda, 7
Hale Makua, 175
Halemaumau, eruption of, 26
Hammamoto, Howard, 82-84
Hargrove house, 96
Hawaii Collection, 55-56
   clubhouse, 87-88
   failure of, 91
   first attempts at marketing, 81-82
   Japanese interest in, 83-84
   land offer, 77-78
   master plan for, 74-75
   proposal for, 63
   purchase contract falls through, 79
   sales projections, 77
   strategy for building, 72
   thoughts on, 183
Hawaii Island house
   as seed for Hawaii Collection, 98
   bathrooms, 128
   and battlefields, 175
   budget over-runs, 132
   buyer for, 179-180
   carpeting, 128
   construction begins, 107
   curved walls causing problems, 112
   decision to live as caretakers, 142
   description of, 101-102
   divorce ceremony on grounds of, 162
   entrance, 134
   estimated cost, 106
   final cost, 137
   final pour of concrete, 127-128
   fireplace, 134
   first attempts to sell, 169
   first thoughts about building, 96-97
   foundation, 111-112
   furniture, 133-134
   glass corners, 118
   hot tub, 132-133
   and Institute of Resonance Therapy, 175-179
   landscaping, 133, 155
   lighting, 129
   planning, 105-107
   problems with building, 109-115
   problems with cabinetry, 132
   problems with furnishings, 124-125
   roof, 117
   and role of Invisible Partners in completion, 137
   sale of, 180
   thoughts on completion of, 137, 183

Hawaii
   first house in, 29
   orders sending Sandy to, 25
   Sandy's attempts at leaving, 26
   thoughts on, 15
Hawken, Paul, 40
heaven, thoughts on, 165-166
Heaven's Gate, and brother, 10
hemi-cycle homes, 98
hepatitis
   first incidence of, 27
   relapse of, 37
Hilo, 25
Hollywood, 8
holon, 177
Honolulu, 25
   one-way ticket to, 28
   Susanne's feelings about, 123
hot coals, walking on, 52-53
hotel and restaurant management, opportunities in, 19
hotel school, 20
Houston, Jean, 95
hunches, confusion about, 49-50
Imperial Hotel, 94
infidelity, Sandy's reaction to Susanne's, 158
informators, 178
Institute, New Millennium, Susanne's idea for, 107
Institute of Noetic Sciences, 147
Institute of Resonance Therapy, 170, 175-176
Introductory Management, job teaching, 30
intuition, thoughts on, 188
Invisible Partners
   and cancer, 172
   and Hawaii Island house, 132, 137
   pressure to build a Wright house, 97
   realization that they exist, 78
   thoughts on, 183-184, 187, 189-190, 192, 193
Janker Clinic, 171
Japan
   experiences in, 27
   interest in Hawaii Collection, 83
   opportunity to go to, 26
   stock market crash in, 91
job offer from bank, 29
Kahuna, 149-150
karma, thoughts on, 188
kinetic art, 96
Koolau Mountains, 29
Kurdendall, Jill, 149
Lakehurst, 25
Leeward Community College, 29

Leonard, George, 44
Lookout Hotel, 18–19
Loveness, Don and Virginia, 98–100
Lutz, Franz, 170, 175–176
Lynch, Robert, 180–181
MacArthur, Dodie, 169, 179–180
Makua, Hale, 149–150
manifestation
  early thoughts on, 49–50
  first experiments with, 39
marketing professor, and effect on Sandy, 17–18
Maryland and Navy orientation school, 24
master plan, Hawaii Collection, 74–75
Mastery, 44
Maunalani Heights, 29
MBA
  plans after receiving, 28
  thoughts on, 17
McKenna, Terence, 123, 143–145
meditation vs. psychedelic drugs, 143
Meighan, Thomas, 6
Miller, Arthur, 87
Mitchell, Edgar, 123, 145–147
Monick, Kerry
  blind date with, 37
  experience with patients, 39
  and Sandy's introduction to New Thought, 38
Monroe, Marilyn, 87
Moody, Raymond, 123
Moody, Raymond, 141–142
Moon, and Edgar Mitchell, 145–147
morphic fields, 177
mother
  appearance, 8
  and cars, 5
  and divorce, 6
  and her parents, 8
Mr. Maui, 82–84
Muqqudam, Faisal, 170
navigation tests, 24
neuro-linguistic programming, 50
New England, Sandy's time in, 18–19
New Millennium Institute, 123, 131
New Port Richey, and grandfather, 6
NLP, see neuro-linguistic programming,
Novelty Theory, 144
offer on land for Hawaii Collection, 77–78
Officers' Candidate School
  experiences at, 21–24
  first awareness of, 19
oranur, 177–178
orders, Sandy's first, 25

orgone, 177–178
orgone shooter, 178
Ouli, 56
Paige, 50–53
parents
  and courtship, 8
  and decision to move west, 8
  and divorce, 9
  and Hollywood, 8
Partners, Invisible see Invisible Partners, 78
Patuxent River, Maryland, and Navy orientation school, 24
Peck Sims Mueller, 91
  Sandy is bought out of, 121–122
Peck, Rich, 31
Pfeiffer, Bruce, 55
pitch to Taliesin for Hawaii Collection, 67–68
Place of Destiny, 56
plan, Hawaii Collection, 74–75
polyamory, Sandy's reaction to, 160–161
Potter, company officer of Charlie Company, 23
Pound, Patti, 56
Precession, 91
professor, and effect on Sandy, 17–18
prostate cancer, Sandy's diagnosis with, 158–160
psychedelic drugs vs. meditation, 143
psychological testing as a child, 15
psychomanteums, 141–142
radionics, 175
Rattenbury, John, 64, 98
  and Kay, 123, 152
Reich, Wilhelm, 175
resonators, 177
Robbins, Tony, 50–53
roof, difficulties building, 117–118
Rosenthal, Ray, 150, 170–171, 175–176
Roswell, theories about, 146
Rote, Kyle and Nina, 82
Russia, travels through, 27
sales projections for Hawaii Collection, 77
Scheef, Wolfgang, 170–171
schizophrenia, and brother, 10
school for Fellowship architects, 65
Schulze, Rick, 180
  and purchase contract, 79
  description of, 57–58
Sekiguchi, Takeschi, 83
Sellers, Tom, 31
Seth, 39
Shamanism, explained by Hank Wesselman, 151
Shimizu Corporation, 83, 87 187

Shoosox, 47–49
Sims, Susanne
  and affair, 156–158
  divorce ceremony, 162
  and feelings about moving away from the city, 123
  and growing unhappiness, 142–143, 155
  and last days of marriage to Sandy, 160–162
  and plans for seminars, 131
  Sandy's reaction to affair, 158
  strain on, 132
socks designed like shoes, 47–49
Spangler, David, 43
Spiritwalker, 149
static art, 96
Stillwater, Virginia, 99
stock market crash in Japan, 91
stranger at financial talk, 13–14
strategy for building the Hawaii collection, 72
stuck energy, 177
Stutz, Jerry, 132
subdivision of Frank Lloyd Wright homes, plans for, 55–56
Susanne see Sims, Susanne
Swager, Jim, 29
Swanson, Gloria, 7
synchronicity, thoughts on, 188, 190–191
Taliesin Fellowship, 58, 152
Taliesin Gates, 88
Taliesin West, 64
Taliesin
  first call to, 55
  presentation to, 63, 67–68
Techniques of Financial Analysis course, 27
techno mass, and Matthew Fox, 151
The Magic of Findhorn, 40
Thompson, Kim, 56–57
time, thoughts on, 189
Timewave Zero, 144
Torweihe, Hans, 105
  admiration for, 137
  problems with, 114
tube socks designed like shoes, 47–49
universe, thoughts on, 189
University of Creation and Spirituality, 151
Viack, Sandy's investment in, 181, 183
Vietnam war, thoughts on, 18
volcano, eruption of, 26
Volkswagen, Mr. Potter and, 23, 24
Voodoo Chiefs, and Hale Makua, 150
Waikapu Mauka Partners
  meeting with, 83
  thoughts on, 187
  visit to Taliesin, 87

Waikiki, 29
Waimea Development Group, 57
war, thoughts on, 18
washing out of OCS, 22
Wesselman, Hank, 123, 149–151
West, Robert, 112
wind, hampering efforts to build the Hawaii Island house, 117–118
Wright, Frank Lloyd
  apartment in Arizona, 65
  first exposure to, 33
  and house in Stillwater, Virginia, 99
  and plans for subdivision, 55–56
  history in Japan, 84
  thoughts on, 183
Wynn, Ed, 6
Yokosuka, 27
Yokouchi, Pundy, 82–84

ACKNOWLEDGMENTS

I am profoundly grateful to John Rattenbury who constantly encouraged me to write. My colleagues, Rick Schulze, Charlie Campbell, Kim Thompson and Tonia Baney were constant companions in the Frank Lloyd Wright adventure.

To Kerry Monick and Susanne Sims, who were integral parts of my development, and provided feedback and useful suggestions to this manuscript.

To my editors, Lana Griffiths and Steven Josephs, who provided me with structure, guidance and support.

To Alice Anne Parker and Mark Travis, who taught me how to tell my story.

To Laura Mueller, who brought her considerable design talent to the creation of the book's look.

To Aaron Wrixon, my insanely thorough proofreader with x-ray vision.

To photographers Carolyn Blake and Jim Cazel.

I shall be eternally indebted to Hans Torweihe and Billy Gwynn for spearheading the creation of an architectural masterpiece.

To Winton Churchill, for his valuable insights and contributions in preparing the book for the internet world. To Randy and Cathy Gilbert for their distribution guidance in this new paradigm.

To Patty Barakat, my partner, who nurtured and supported my daily progress, and whose knowledge of healthy practices gave me a new lease on life.

I would also like to thank one particular organization that helped me in my formative years: the Boy Scouts of America. Learning to align with the forces of nature, both in physical experience and thinking patterns, instilled in me the seeds of independence, curiosity, and perseverance; these gave me the self-confidence to explore and face the challenges of later life.

And to the legion of supporters who made this journey a continuous and gracious adventure, my enduring thanks.

ABOUT SANDY SIMS

Have you felt overwhelmed and somewhat powerless with the pace of change, the uncertainty, and how to cope? Have you worked hard to obtain a goal, only to realize that it did not bring you the joy you thought it would? Have you wished you had a more useful point of view? This is exactly the place Sandy found himself, in a small Honolulu start-up advertising agency many years ago. Although considering himself quite average, he had cultivated one particularly useful trait — an abiding curiosity, and the desire to check out many of our culturally accepted patterns for himself.

In this autobiographical journey Sandy reveals how a career and health crisis opens doors to an expanded reality where he meets remarkable people. He learns about our greater powers to manifest, which he decides to consciously test, upping the ante incrementally, ultimately becoming immersed in the legacy of America's greatest architect, Frank Lloyd Wright. In so doing he discovers that we have been more the architects of our lives than we think: that what we call luck, chance, and coincidence are more design than not, and that "Invisible Partners" can make our ordinary lives extraordinary, no matter what the situation, when we are willing to engage, trust and nurture the partnership.

This is a watershed time in history, an era in which we are becoming more aware of how powerful our minds are. It is a time when not only how we use our minds, but what we think about, will determine the elegance of our lives.

Reginald Sanderson (Sandy) Sims was raised and educated in the South. After serving as a Naval Officer and finishing graduate business school, he followed a dream to live in Honolulu, where he built one of Hawaii's largest and most successful advertising agencies. He resides in Hawaii and San Miguel de Allende, Mexico.

After writing this book
I had many people suggest
that a workbook distilling brief
but essential thinking patterns
into easy-to-do exercises
would be extremely helpful.

CREATIVE THINKING FOR THE 21ST CENTURY: AN EXPERIENTIAL GUIDEBOOK.

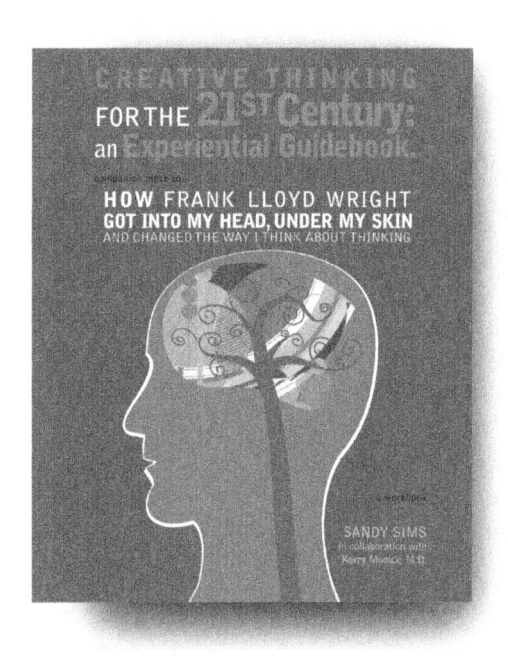

Available through bookstores and electronic retailers.